"Marquis Who's Who Lifetime Achievement Award"

"The work exuberantly credits God as the source of truth and glory."

—BlueInk

CRAIG CARPENTER DOWNER

WONDER

STREAMS OF THE SOUL

VOLUME 2

WONDER STREAMS OF THE SOUL:
Volume 2

Copyright © 2024 by Craig Carpenter Downer. All rights reserved.

Printed in the United States of America

2024.10.26

PRELUDE

<u>Wonder Streams of the Soul</u> arose from a beautiful desire to share the best and highest in life. This is Volume 2 of my ground-breaking book in which you will find some extraordinary revelations, exquisite and exciting poems and remarkably profound and insightful passages, many of which are vividly illustrated. Since a tender age, I have experienced thoughts and feelings that seemed beyond the ordinary and bursting to be expressed. One such I call life's "spiritual evolution" taking place both individually and collectively. With the blessings of an extensive arts and sciences education at some of the world's finest universities (loving thanks to my dear parents) and through intense and sweeping introspection, in my book I have combined diverse knowledge with personal insights that are penetrating and even transcendent.

As a student I started jotting down major points during lectures and field trips and this habit continued throughout my life. Through long practice, this habit of copious note taking led to a heightened awareness of my experiences, both outward and inward. I have become increasingly aware of a rhythm of thoughts and feelings, a web of interrelations, and a great melodic onward flow within my own as well as all interrelated life. Repeatedly revising my verbal expression has allowed me to more perfectly conceive the brilliant *spiritual evolution* that unites all and fulfills us all.

<u>Wonder Streams of the Soul</u> and the inner awakening it impels ties in with all Life's salvation. I see my unusually varied poems, passages and illustrations as lifebuoys thrown out to my fellow humans too many of whom seem to be sinking into a dark sea of meaninglessness. If these poems stir you deeply and serve to elevate you to a finer attunement to life's true beauty, then I shall rest content that my purpose has been achieved. If my book can do this even for a few fellow souls striving forth here on planet Earth, then it shall not have been written in vain.

Coming from a family of avid readers to whom words have been like daily food and drink, I highly recommend as a lifetime pursuit learning to read better and more, for rightly combined and appreciated, words can provide the very keys to salvation. And the reading of them is inextricably linked to the generating of them. Furthermore, they must be complemented by actions that effect certain enlightened changes that words foretell. Words are an integral part of life's equation. To paraphrase Poe in his "The Poetic Principle": 'by achieving in words a more perfect expression of those greater truths one awakens to in one's ongoing experience, one gains a more clear and perfect realization thereof'. So, let us commence our journey. Freely received and freely given, with Charity for everyone. Welcome!

TABLE OF CONTENTS

LIFE AND DEATH, LIFE'S MEANING

Photo by author, of a Honeysuckle vine in blossom, early morning. Spring, 2019.

BACK ALIVE! (7/30/2020 while hiking north shore Lake Tahoe, afternoon in the garden)

Life comes *back alive*
in a positive way
when we
stop taking for granted:
things,
and what's more *places,*
and what's more *times,*
and what's more *beings,*
and the interconnected *events*
that link these all
according to their hierarchies
and their origins
and their ends
and that Precious Restored State
to which all these tend.
Praise God! Amen.

DIMENSIONS OF CONSCIOUSNESS: A POEM CONCERNING LIFE'S MEANING (Spring, 2003)

So many dimensions of consciousness,
boxes contained within yet bigger boxes,
spheres: within yet greater spheres,
there out there, in here,
to be discovered are
by each and every one of us,
as by ALL of us together.
… Parallel universes, as it were, we are,
yet ever one throughout…

Consider the vast and twinkling stars,
most of which: whole galaxies,
we see, we hear, from the surface
of home planet Earth,
in whose inner depths also
many mysterious secrets
yet lie to unlock their truths,
when Time and Fate:
the Hand of God reveals!

Correspondingly, so many dimensions of consciousness
each individual being—each one of us—passes through
by means of birth, by means of death,
and that which corresponds
in the higher world
to this our worldly life,
more precisely by means of
attachment and detachment,
including sex and violence,
refinement and again growing heavy,
and all such dramatic transitions,
though there are those so peaceful,
and each with its own special
yet interrelated reason

—yet with all this the cycle
ever and again is reborn,
not just to cycle, but
to spiral forth discovering…

… Related at each moment,
as throughout all such,
with each and every so-called "other"
parallel-evolving being unique,
each a point of consciousness,
and one who shall not desist
until it reaches the very Highest
Dimension subsuming all lesser ones
… and many a weaving back
and forth there is between, among.

Each point of consciousness over Time
this Goal Sublime pursues.
—Oh! Great wonder of life, of world,
of World of worlds
... thus, to be *So Free,*
for, thus, to rise So High,
ever by grace and to the Glory Divine!

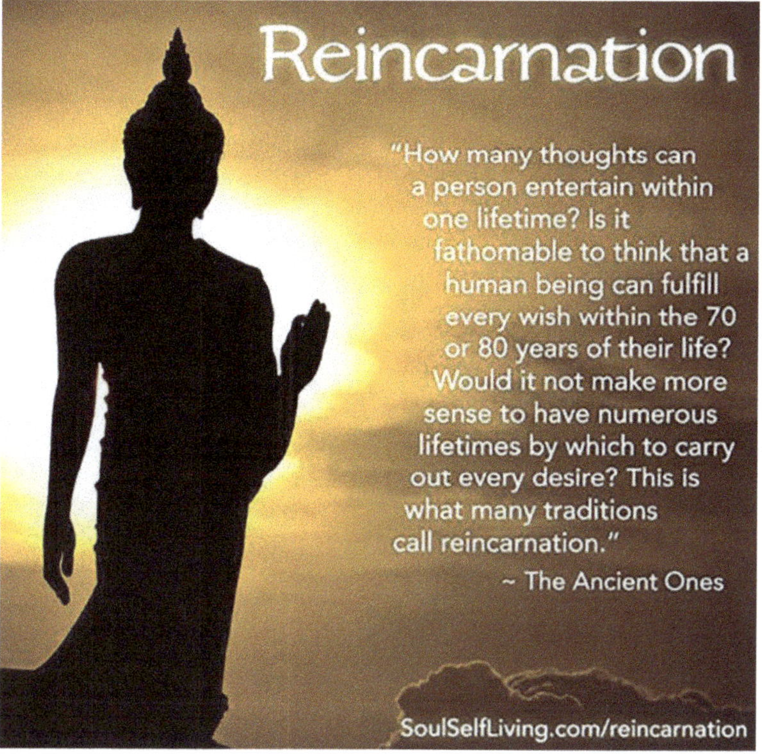

Image from Soul Self Living, Reincarnation, soulselfliving website.

CYCLING (1995)

Oh! To think of all
the people who are born,
then "max" out in life,
fade away and die,
lying down in their graves,
bones and flesh returning
to the cosmic cycling
of materials and energies
and their souls likewise
to the cosmic cycles of immortal Spirit.
- Aye! 'T is a contemplation most magnificent!
Is it not?
Surely so it is. Praise God!
And Hallelujah! shout.

LIFE OR DEATH? (2/27/2001)

"Life or Death?" is a question
of where you place your attention,
of where you fix your identity
and your heart's affection,
of where you focus your mind.
So, let this be upon
God, the Perfect and the Whole,
not upon worldly transient states,
ever imperfect and un-whole,
for these but serve
to point to God
—whose name we do forever praise!

TWO THOUGHTS ON DEATH (12 March, 2001)

Death is the great delusion!
And so is Birth!
Both the great appearing
and disappearing act are,
of the spirit into
and out of the flesh
and the world.
Be not by this trick fooled,
for the Godly spirit lives on,
neither created, nor destroyed!
Surely not. Praise God! Praise God!

LIFE (12 March, 2001)

This I have learned about Life:
that inherent in the very continuum
of Time we each experience
in our own unique, yet interrelated fashion,
is the very composition of thought-feeling
that leads to **TRUTH!**

YOUNG (1995)

The one
who can still look forward in life
to its better part,
or realization yet to come,
had not grown old but remains
ever so young,
no matter how many rounds the Sun
this Earth has flown
since one's present life's
birthing dawn.
Surely it is so.
Praise God! Amen.

Photo of author at 14 months of age, by Little Folks Studio in Reno, Nevada.

A CHILD (8 March, 2001)

"This statement only applies to a relative minority of people, actually, and certainly not those of my immediate family—my wonderful mother and father, sister and brother! I imagine that everyone has felt this way at some point in their life … a bit misunderstood."

I entered into this world
a child laden with noble sentiment,
full of noble love,
for all my fellow spirits,
in all the diverse forms of creation.
But many have been
the harsh receptions
to my presence here,
the cold shoulders and
the indifferent or down right mean
treatments. Yet, I am not

bitter because of this,
but through this have learned
all the more to confide
in Heaven and in God,
for truly He has opened
such vast and wondrous
vistas unto my animal and plant kin
as well as to my fellow man.
Truly so He has.
Praise God! Amen. Amen.

The author, Craig, on Venice Beach, California, after delivering his World's Endangered Species speech. Photo by Cait A. Kennedy of West Hollywood. Late November, 2017.

Poem to Myself, 2017

Tell him he'll see
"we love you"
written in the stars,
that he has only to
go out and look up,
to peer into
those pure desert skies,
to respire deeply
those pure desert airs…
those stars, those skies, those airs
wherever he may roam,
and to know
that we're still here with him,
ever have been and will remain,
whether he realizes it or not
–and to fear not,
for — Lo!
I am with you always
even unto the ends of the Earth!

YESTERDAY (Winter, 2001)

Yesterday,
and the shadows of my memory
are not shadows merely,
but very lights that
do brighten my way!

… The Beatles' song of this title
has a compelling unity,
touching familiar notes
in many of us,
though four decades nearly
have passed since
it was first sung
by our bright companions.

—Yes, it is
a song that lingers,
as all my yesterdays
do linger on!
Yet, for this very reason,
these are integral
to the here and now!
I hear them still!
And for this very reason
a pertinent, timely lesson,
they must bear!

Image from Yin Yang - Ancient Wisdom. From wakeupworld website.

PLAY OF OPPOSITES (2/27/2001)

I find the play of opposites in life:
Dullness: sharpness, weakness: strength,
viciousness: virtue,
as this is experienced
in all possible ways
in this we call life,
as a necessary interplay
and being like that
great and fateful wheel
which moveth up and down,
forward and backward
—and for this very reason
goeth forth unto all perfection
and wholeness, unto God.
Truly so it rolleth forth
unto all Heavenly Restoration.
Praise God! Amen. Amen.

Photo by author of purplish golden-colored sunset over Lake Tahoe
with pines in foreground. October, 2013.

OF HALLOWEEN SUN AND PUMPKINS (10/1996)

I write:
of Halloween sun and pumpkins,
and learning to treat life with subtle art,
by asking that further question,
in "polite" society seldom dared,
by mixing witches and sorcerers with priests,
ghosts and goblins with incarnate ones,
by magical spells
—by facing grim Death
squarely in the face
and therein discerning a Parody of "life,"
even the humorous side thereof.
But the joke's on us,
for we mortals are the butt
that's just burned out,
the presumptuous stick
that's just gone flat,
while immortal souls,
those dearly departed,
behold our worldly attachments

and the "death" to which
these inevitably do lead
from just beyond the Veil
(of Earthly Delusion).
For they wear no worldly
masks, as we mortals do,
nor to these masks
themselves attach,
neither inside nor out.
They seek not to hide
in any way, shape, or form,
nor do they even generally try
—though some may from time to time!
They fly on white witches' broomsticks
high up into a moon-lit sky,
there at last to greet
a dawning New Day
… and this mellowly glowing,
Halloween sun
and all the marvelously varied "pumpkins"

its light reveals
in magically arrayed hues
of fantastic reds, oranges,
yellows, and goldens
—and has a place here too
most majestic purple—
one with the subtle art of
all God's holy spectrum
that's all encompassing, all unveiling,
from out all the mists of Time
(we all have lived),
revealing this world
according to diverse lights,
according to all interweaved times,
including this specially
wrinkled Halloween one,
so as to grasp this
ever forward cycling Spiral
that is the true Life
we live, we share,
and every have and
ever shall—Eternal!—
including all countless critters wherever.
And by this I mean the spirits thereof.
… Aye! Here's a subtle
art worthy to describe!!
Praise ye the all-radiant God!

Photo by author of recently helicopter-driven and captured wild stallions who now await their uncertain fate in the BLM holding pens north of Reno, Nevada. Note their air of indignation and even despair, but also a glimmer of hope that I might deliver them from this dreary captivity and set them free in the natural world again. (October, 2013)

ONE HATES TO DIE, A LOOSELY KNIT BURTONELLE (3/21/2003)

One hates to die	before one's time
before the soul's	very purpose Divine
for being here	upon this plane
unique, in fact, indispensable	has been fulfilled
and it's such a shame	to see one's life's blood spilled
upon the dry desert	sands of indifference.
For the inspired genius	of true Action
a.k.a.	Relation,
the Completion	shall not forever be denied
—Oh! Great, as yet	unfulfilled Potentiality
within Each one of us	as within All
Praise God!	Forever and ever.
In life	each individual ever

in one or another way	comes to face
the consequences	of his/her/its choices
and through this process	we all come
face to face	with our own true selves
however bitterly betimes	and with each
further meeting	this we are ever doing.
How extraordinary	these quirky
appointments in time	may seem
yet how very ordinary	indeed!
You know that	to recognize relations
wheresoever you may roam	in a truly benign and inspired way
— Aye! — 't is to awaken	so much that has
for far too long	lain latent
but that still	shall have its day
even in this present dawning	now a-breaking
both without and within	all this called life,
all this called	you and me
and she and he	and we!

TO THE DEARLY DEPARTED, AN *APOSTROPHE* (9/27/2003)

To you
who are yet with me,
though perhaps not so much
anymore in the flesh,
yet in part
and for this very reason
all the more recognized
in pure spirit,
for by my own self-
reflected mind and heart detected,
yet, within Beingness'
ever greater dimension
—greater than the mere physical world
and all that it contains
or would contain,
I say:
God bless and God speed
you on your way,
and may the spirit of
true, for compassionate, Love,
not just the worldly possessive kind,
ever guide us all on
—there where we're finally bound,
to that Great Celestial Home
upon which all
separate, unique paths converge,
as all the minds and hearts and wills
of all souls
upon God's Holy
and Ever Living Truth!

RESTORATION (9/2/1999)

Those happy times,
those happy places,
and all the relations therein known,
so quickly dashed to pieces,
by Time and Fate,
or so it seems
—remember them well,
that they may be
restored some day
within one or more
of those many lives
which you have yet
in store to live!

Image from Timsy - YouTube.

DESTINY (8/8/1999)

One knows where
one's destiny has called,
presently calls,
and in future times
still will call;
to what lives yet to be lived,
to what special roles: played,
to which future, present, and past loves
- Oh! so precious these -
all to further realize.
Oh! Wondrous spiritual life!
Ever by grace and to the glory On High!

QUEST (9/10/1999)

The process of life in its deeper sense
is a quest for meaning,
truth, unity, interconnection,
beauty, wholeness and perfection,
in which is to be found
true fulfillment, happiness, joy, love.
This goes on
in the true life of
each and every individual,
consciously evolving being.
And it is my great joy
in this my present life
to speak through my writings
to the very heart and soul of such.
Praise God! And Hallelujah! shout.

ANIMATION (9/2/1999)

All that bespeaks *animation*
bespeaks life's great truth,
its abiding spirit,
not the mere physical machine,
taken in and of itself!
Surely not!
Praise God! And Hallelujah! shout.

Photo by author of an amazing Albatross gliding over brisk ocean at mouth of Doubtful Sound, South Island, New Zealand. May, 2019.

DEATH (9/2/2003)

Aging and death
are figments of the
mortal view of life.
In truth we
all live forever,
ever have, do, and shall,
one in Space,
one in Time,
and, most of all,
one in Spirit
—Oh! Holy Spirit
all transcending!
Truly it is so.
Praise God! Amen.

Photo by author, from inner Doubtful Sound, South Island, New Zealand. Shows awesome vision
 of light descending over jagged, cloudy peaks and suggesting the opening of Heaven. May, 2019.

HEAVENLY REASON (7/27/1999)

Recognizing the Heavenly reason
for each new, as old, aspect of
worldly life, for each
new, as old, experience
—all aspects and experiences every being
so perfectly interconnected—
one is restored in faith,
uplifted in inspired belief
unto the very Highest who is God!
Truly so one is.
Praise God! I say, Praise God!
And Hallelujah! shout.

ATMOSPHERE (7/25/2003)

Mystically aware
of the great atmosphere of Time
that surrounds
each spell of conscious attachment,
or detachment,
I become aware
of life's higher
sense and purpose,
meaning and glory.
Truly so I do!
Praise God! And shout Hallelujah!

THE PURE, TRUE LIFE (7/18/1999)

Be not confounded, oh! my soul,
that the ideal life
seems not to jive
with the worldly manifest one,
for the spirit of life
exists upon a higher plane;
and though all
manifest here below
is a consequence
of its spiritual cause,
still the wheels of causation
can at times most slowly grind.
So, just keep your faith,
your attention fixed
upon the great Divine within,
existing beyond
all the world of mere
external manifestation,
and that ever "supercedes"
and outstrips this,
for such is within the miracle
of the evolving spirit,
who in ever more
perfectly awakening
consciousness does move,
that whole transformed
worlds of the future
become effected through
the wondrous powers
of our own true dreams,
visions, Heavenly inspirations
that are life's true work
and that especially go on within
one's own truest, for inmost, self,
whom the world cannot touch.
Truly not.
Praise God!
Praise God!

DEATH (7/14/1999)

This I've learned about worldly life:
that death at last brings peace,
and that there is a great beauty
then that arises from each
life that's been lived,
experienced upon the manifest plane,
as it resolves itself
with all that's come and gone
before in past time,
and, so, goes on to
that every greater
resolution in times future,
until all that has been written
also has been experienced, lived,
and, so, it's true meaning
fully learned, appreciated
—ever by grace
and to the glory of God!

Photo by author, showing young maple with brilliant golden and purplish leaves, backlit. Near Virginia City, Nevada. Autumn, 2016.

AUTUMN LEAVES—A *DODITSU* (10/24/2004)

Autumn leaves so cool and fresh,
about them there's a hint of death,
as owl hoots weirdly nearby
Paradoxic'ly.

LIFE'S PAUSES (2/12/2005)

It is in life's pauses,
one of which is so-called death itself,
that we are given time to reflect upon
that which we have just lived
and, so, then prepare ourselves for
the next wave:
our next new, more perfect life.
Praise God!

Photo by author, of sun rising over Pine Nut Mountains, western Nevada. Ca. 2015.

NOT FOR GRANTED—LIFE! (March 2nd, 2005, birthday of Alice Marie Gottschalk Downer, mother of author and in tribute to her.)

The character of each one
is vast and deeply drawn!
And there's a meantness in all this
—in each appointment, hers or his!
And all this hails the Dawn!

How many times one looks at life
as if there's no true sense,
but taking time to feel, reflect,
discovers promise, truth inflects
—reanimates credence!

Take not for granted any being!
We all are here as one!
In spirit we do ever share
life's wondrous purpose, meaning, dare!
And God shines as our Sun!

His lessons come in many forms,
in places and in times,
in meant encounters with all kin,
as music comes from out the din,
discord transforms to rhymes!

And each pure soul has grace unique
—such wonders to perform!
O'er all the ages—many lives
and loves and deaths—*being* forth still strives
—*Creation to Transform!*

EACH LIFE ON EARTH BEGINS WITH A FEELING (8/31/2020)

A remarkable observation about
All Living Creatures on Earth,
Or elsewhere in this Universe,
Is that these are each and all
Manifest Expressions of Spirit,
And that each such
Begins with a Feeling,
A Conception,
And that this then
Leads to its Manifest Expression
Both within and to all the World of
Fellow Manifest Expressors
Implanted in this Matrix
Of a so-called "inanimate" planet—
But that is, in a more subtle way,
Also Animate, involved with Spirit.
Now, in this seemingly simple,
Straight forward statement,
Is contained a Principle
So Profound, so Universal,
That to realize it fully
Is to be Transformed
And then to oneself transform,
Because Uplifting
All this Life and World—
And really All Who Oneself Surround.
Praise God! Amen.

INDIVIDUAL EXPRESSIONS

Photo by author of two exquisite wild horses from Steens Mountain Herd Management Area, Oregon in Spring of 2009.

THE BODY (3/13/2001)

The inherent logic in the body
as an adaptation for
survival in this world
is beautiful to behold,
for something more than just
physical survival
and reproduction is involved.
Yes! Something more,
and which no mere thing is,
and that all things subsumes.
— Oh! Holy spirit
evolving back from the Fall
and unto God! Praise God!

FEATURES (2/23/2001)

What unique and special experiences
your features sculpted have
… your own unique and special knowledge,
elicited from out your own
true inner depths
OF ALL POSSIBILITY AND TIME?!
Ask of yourself and each other
this question well, oh! my soul,
that you the soul-smothering
veil of worldly delusion
may pierce!
For, thus, you'll perceive beyond,
for so conceiving.
Praise God! Amen. Amen.

Craig Carpenter Downer, photo collections, including one of himself by wild horse advocate Bernie Roghers and all the others including the 4 Month old Tapir taken by the author. The "stone horse" was taken in the Three Fingers Wild Horse HMA in SE Oregon. – all © Craig C. Downer.

Photo by author, of sunset over Sierra Nevada,
from northwestern Reno. Taken August 9, 2015.

AURA (1995)

Each place has its own special aura,
or vibration, as does each person,
each animal, each plant.
Yet none are separate!
No nation stands apart!
No continent can
within itself be contained!
For we all props
to one another are;
and out of our
very relationships
do fashion our identities.
Oh! Sacred Forest
of kindred spirits,
ancient in Time,
yet ever renewing,
ever rebirthing,
ever young!
Praise God! Amen. Amen

INDIVIDUAL UNIQUENESS (9/21/2000)

Each soul decides
for him/her self
which route to follow
according to the inner wisdom
of his/her own true
heart and mind.
He/she knows
what karmic debts
he/she has to pay
and wherein his/her
own unique destiny
does lie—
one unique,
yet, paradoxically,
of indispensable relation
to that of all fellow souls,
for this by dint
of a very individual and
Divinely appointed
Singularity.

*Palomino Eye Photo –© Craig C.
Downer*

TRUE DEFINITION (8/7/1999)

Being without a friend,
I learn to appreciate
the true definition of "friend."
Without "love," as the world calls it,
I learn to appreciate again
the true meaning of *Love*.
And, so, it is
with all aspects of life:
virtue, strength, intelligence, wisdom:
we learn better to appreciate these
from their outward absence,
for then we as individuals
must call upon
our own inner selves
in order to supply
these absolute necessities
for the sustenance of life
—for then, wondrously, miraculously,
we find these to lie *within*.
Truly so we do.
Praise God! Amen. Amen.

Painting from Pioneers Artwork by Lacabezaenlasnubes, from artsider website.

PIONEER (8/2/1999)

Be a pioneer in spirit,
searching out new perspectives
of universal truth,
that all may gain
by your daring.
Likewise do not refrain
from following in those times
when, similarly, you are led.
Praise God! I say, Praise God!

TRUE POSSESSION (8/3/1999)

What greater possession
hath any man
than his own inward self
and experience?
Such as makes us all equals,
though each following
his/her/its own unique way,
leading both to the
realization of one's own true self
and to that of all others -
all ways converging
upon the self-same
Truth Divine
Throughout the whole eternity
of our becoming.
For such is life!
Truly so it is.
Praise God! Amen.

BRILLIANT SELF-IMAGE (8/2/1999)

People fashion
their own self-image around
many things,
but the Greatest Truth,
and all life's motion
towards this Wholeness and perfection,
is ever testing these
transient identifications,
or self-images.
So, it is best
to be aware of the process
and to seek to recognize as real
only that which is perfect and whole,
regardless of how
imperfect or un-whole
may be your and others'
current realization of such.
—Surely only the very best
shall in the end be attained
and give us true
and lasting Peace!

CHANNELER (7/3/1999)

Be ye a channeler
from the ever
higher Heaven, oh! my soul,
unto this world
where you find yourself in body,
that an uplifter
you may be
and not a degrader;
a blessing,
and not a curse!
Surely so be ye!
Praise God! And set me free!

HAPPENING (7/27/1999)

If you would know
the true happening of life,
look within
your very own self.
Praise God!

KNOWLEDGE OF THE SOUL (7/17/1999)

To possess knowledge of the soul
and knowledge in relation to the soul
is more valuable
than all mere worldly life
and its offerings,
but perceived in relation to the immortal soul,
this same worldly life
takes on enhanced meanings,
is revived, for known in relation
to its own true and transcendent cause,
its Heavenly super-nature
all in relationship to God!

AVOID WORLDLY MANIPULATORS (7/17/1999)

Be not a mindless,
heartless, will-less puppet
of the vested moneyed interests
who have little interest in your soul
and its purpose for being here,
but only look shamelessly
to their own worldly
self-aggrandizement!
Be not so beholden,
but, rather, take stock within
yourself and in all
that God has given you!
In other words, stand up,
be brave and free and pure,
for this is the way to life
—all else death is. Praise God!

Photo by BLM worker of author on left presenting petition to Stop Excessive Roundups and his book to Edwin Roberson at Secretary of Interior office, Washington, late January, 2014. Part of author's campaign to restore wild horses and burros.

STRIVE (7/17/1999)

Strive to develop
sensitivity to life's
higher cause and meaning
that you may become
pure in heart
by questioning your motivations
and outlook upon life
that, thus, ye may learn to see
and in all ways
to perceive God.

UNITY, UNIVERSE, AND RELATION

A CHALLENGE CALLED RELATION: A *QUASI-SONNETTELLA* (August, 2001)

You know that Vain Science makes a "Religion"
out of arrogant Materialism,
and Thoughtless Technocracy to this does join
to bring Man Up, but put Life Down—Bad Schism!
—Yet Life's True Story's not so falsely written,
for something Greater from the Heart does dawn,
for within a Greater Tapestry knit in
our fine lives have been—and are yet still drawn,
according to a challenge called *Relation*
—by High Order of Love's Plan: ***PERFECTION!***

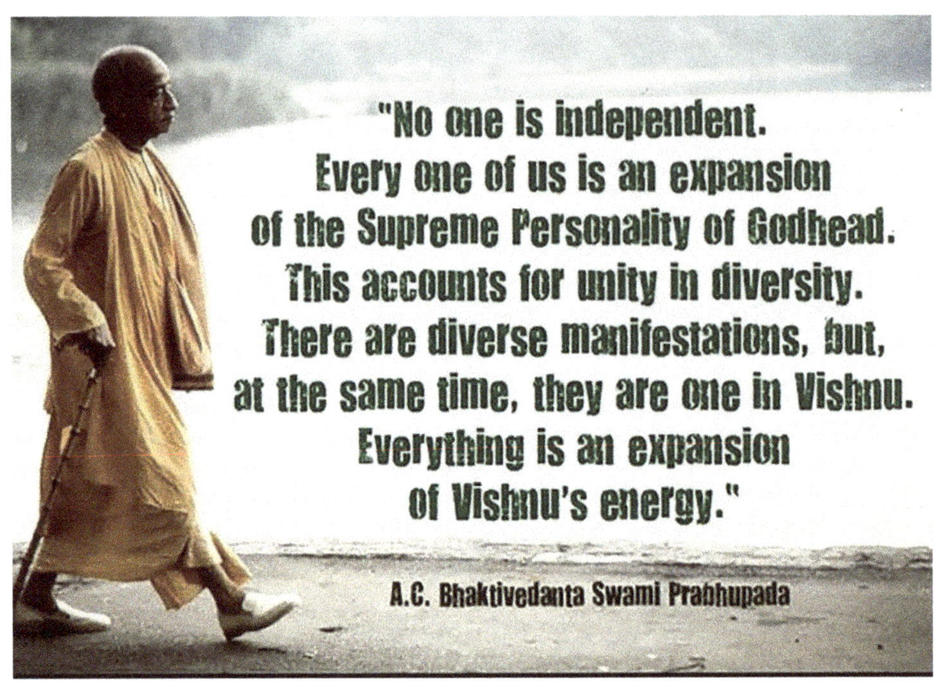

"According to the US Census Bureau as of 2022, there are nearly 8 billion humans living on the Earth today. So the human species has added around 2 billion humans to the face of the earth in 23 years!" Image from 62 Best Quotes And Sayings About Unity, from askideas website.

THE MANY AND THE ONE: A PRAYER

(April, 1999, La Bonita, Sucumbios, Ecuador)

I write a prayer
about The Many and The One!
And, you know,
there's now Six Billion
souls incarnate in human form
upon this beautiful,
but much fraught Earth!
And that's not counting
all the other souls who
in other diverse forms
are wrought.
Yet, you know,
however arbitrary worldly barriers
seem to be imposed
between and among us all,

as Heaven knows,
according to God's Perfect Law,
we all ever
One in Spirit are!
And those relations
seemingly the most impossible
and remote
to our limited
mortal view of life,
in fact,
the most beautiful become,
for these correspondences
are the most Eternal,
the most Sublime!

Photo by author. Sunrise over Lake Tahoe,
taken from Meeks Bay, California (2005).

THE SUN (from *The Spiritual Evolution…* 1981, book by the author, see excerpts from
this amazing book given later)

In the midst of smothering darkness,
in all its holy starkness,
there burns a holy light,
kept ever by His might.
Yet, though it be night,
't is dawn to me,
holding no fright,
but ecstasy!
There is a faint light,
all-permeating as Divine Love,
which sublimes to a height,
this world to the far home of the Dove!
In this dawn I want to awaken,
my eternal desire, constantly!
I want to be taken,
there, to home, to be free!
Where everyone is one,
a Glorious Sun!

TOUCHING (2/14/2001)

Each touches ALL,
and ALL touches each.
Such is the great,
interfused reality of Life,
as ever onward we evolve,
self-perfecting and thereby perfecting all
who with us evolve
… that is in Time
this process of recovery
of all that was lost at the Fall,
this reawakening to
that great and Glorious Perfection
that ever is and is Life's Truth!
Truly so. Praise God, forsooth!

FELLOW SOUL (3/13/2001)

See each fellow soul,
as well as yourself,
in his/her/its
present condition
as integral to life's
great evolving story,
as not limited merely
to certain known
present and past states,
but as ever moving
unto its own,
and all our shared,
Perfect Realization,
as ever Forth out of Darkness
and into the Heavenly Light
that looms we all do go,
back from the Fall
and gloriously unto God.
Praise God!

Image from Threadstock illustrations, 70555933, from Dreamstime website.

THREADS (3/3/2001)

Beautiful is the realization
of those long-lost threads
of time and experience
one once lived
then seemingly forgot,
as these weave back,
themselves again knot
into one's conscious life,
as they present themselves once more
like long-lost strangers
and for reasons beyond mere mortal law.
Truly so. Praise God! Praise God!

THE UNIVERSAL RELATION (March, 2001)

Contemplating the *universal relation*
wherever I do roam,
I think of *Love*
and all it *means!*
Considering all
the vast possibilities
that unfold
throughout the whole of Time,
I am transported
beyond just this one
mortal experience
unto that Greater Life
all these tiny lives **subsumes.**
Yes, I think of
the True and Universal Love
that awaits *both me*
and us.
Truly so I do.
Praise God!
And Hallelujah! shout.

THOUGHTS ON UNITY (3/10/2001)

Whether we like it or not,
or choose to recognize,
the great sublime fact
of life is that
we are all ever
one in spirit,
one in the great transcendent,
Heavenly dimension. And even
the physical realm,
which is the spirits' effect,
or manifest expression,
teaches us this great Truth,
as in all Space and in all Time,
and by all types of things
and manifest relations,
our sublime UNITY IN SPIRIT
is proven. Truly so it is.
Praise God! Amen. Amen.

… Take the experience of life as it comes, oh! my soul,
for though there appears to be
a trillion, trillion, trillion, trillion,
individual souls in the Universe according
to the exterior view of life,
in Truth, we all ever
ONE IN SPIRIT are,
all in relationship to God.
And this is the only
sane view of life to have.

… True happiness in life
is learning to appreciate what comes one's way,
for its universal fitting and Heavenly
meantness, or intent. Now,
this amounts to
not taking life for granted!

… Beautiful is the remote correspondence
between and among all similar and seemingly
dissimilar kinds: of mountains, of oceans, of
plants, of animals,
of relatively impure and pure of conscience spirits
—and we are all this or have been or will yet be—
of beings, wherever, whenever, whomsoever,
and of whatsoever manifest form and behavior.

Truly so magnificent this is.
Praise God! I say, Praise God!

Photo by author, of subtly hued golden sunset take in western Nevada, probably Reno. Recent.

TRANSITION (4/15/2003)

Each seething sunset slipping away
such a soothing significance portrays:
the end of this day's special dream,
the beginning of this night's,
as Poe's "silken, sad, uncertain… curtains" fall
and Heavens again alight
with myriad twinkling stars
and galaxies so far out,
one has to reach very deep *within*
truly to know them!
Praise God! Amen.

CONNECTIONS (9/14/1999)

Subtle connections
exist in spirit
between and among
all our diverse lives
that, though often
seemingly unconnected,
yet, in truth,
are always interconnected,
and in so many, many ways,
concrete and subtle,
now apparent or now unrecognized,
and that all mutually complemental
shall ultimately be judged,
for known—for lived! Praise God!

Photo by author, of five-year-old Salasacan girl, above Ambato, Ecuador. 1993.

FACES (9/1/2003)

Reminiscing upon all the places
and all the faces
I have known,
by some magical blessing,
these coalesce as one,
bringing me alive,
prompting me to face
those future faces
and places and times
that I shall yet know
—and with such bright eyes
and such keen ears, *et cetera!*
Praise God!

TAKING STOCK (8/23/1999)

Look not with jealousy upon others,
but rather take stock in
what God has given you
throughout all times;
and know that we all
related are in life's
great and universal becoming.
For truly it is so.
Praise God! I say, Praise God!
And Hallelujah! shout.

UNITY (8/16/1999)

There is a unity to life, world
such that each event, experience, expression
is universally recorded,
registered with all places, times,
and, most of all,
fellow spiritual ones.
And for this reason
there is no escaping
our responsibility
to one and to all,
including to each one's
very own true self.
Truly such unity there is.
Praise God! And Hallelujah! shout.

Photo from Royalty-Free photo, Dragon Flame poster, from pickpik website.

SPIRIT MIRRORS (8/8/1999)

Each fellow being
is a mirror of yourself,
showing forth to you
that same essential
spirit you are and who
one with very universal existence is:
the discoverer and knower
—the realizer of truth!

THE PART AND THE WHOLE (9/7/1999)

Each part depends upon the whole.
The whole depends upon each part.
Each part is indispensably related to
each and every other part.
Each one is inseparable from the whole.
All related is,
ordered according to
very highest priority.
Godly Spirit is Highest Truth.
All that is taken
as existing apart from Godly Spirit
is misconception, perversity—the worldly lie!
This know and go free
to rise up On High!
Surely so do.
Praise God! Hallelujah!

MUTUALISM (7/31/1999)

We do not live
to the denial, or put down,
of one another,
but, rather, to the confirmation
and uplifting thereof
—ever by grace
and to the Glory of God!

ATTACK (7/19/2003)

To attack any fellow spirit
is to open oneself
for counterattack.
This is logical.
The resolution will ever
involve damage
yet eventual
healing to both sides,
not just the one
first attacked.
And, thus, it is
that we'll both
be the better off for it.
And ultimately even
learn to better
get along. Truly so.
Praise God! Amen.

RELATED (7/17/1999)

Each life is ever related
to each other life.
All lives form
a great togetherness.
Never forget this,
oh! my soul!…
the interconnections…
how related we all are
to each other
and how all in life tends
to the very greatest of all ends—
in truth, a return to the "beginning"…
unto the very *Source Divine!*
Praise God! I say, Praise God! Amen.

OPPOSITE POINT OF VIEW (7/12/1999)

To the vulgar way of viewing life,
the soul of life is worthless;
in fact, the less
soul-realizing souls the better
from their dark and dense
and unloving point of view,
caught in a fetish of sin.
But to the spiritually enlightened soul,
all the very opposite is true;
and this is, indeed, the truth!
Praise God! And Hallelujah! shout.

WITH THE WHOLE (2/8/2005)

Ever strive
to identify with the whole,
not just the part,
of life
—of beingness—
oh! my soul,
whoever you may be,
that both you and we
together may rise,
ever by grace
and to the glory On High!

THE WORLD, SOCIETY

Image from Connect Your Microcosm with the Macrocosm, from dailysprk website.

MICROCOSM: MACROCOSM (3/9/2001)

In the microcosm,
the macrocosm is prophesied.
And, so, in each episode of Time,
the Whole Story of Time
prophesied is!
And even so, in the life of each soul
is inherent the life of all souls!
Praise God!

ELEMENTS (2/28/2001. Read at Shumaker College, UK, Spring, 2004, by Xiomara Navas-Carbo from Ecuador. She worked with author on Andean Tapir project.)

All the elements for Perfection
are before us in the present,
but we each must learn
to recognize how they rightly
fit together, in what
just juxtaposition and proportion,
wondrously symmetrical as pertains
to all aspects of Creation.
—And for this reason,
there is **Time!**
Truly so there is.
Praise God! I say, Praise God!
Amen.

SOCIETY (2/26/2001)

A society is characterized
as much by what it ignores
as by what it recognizes.
And often what it ignores
is the greater portion
of God's Whole and Perfect Truth!
So just take care, oh! my soul,
to, in pure honesty
—that is the spirit of Love—
toward this Pure and Holy Truth
go forth,
for, thus, are you free—
ever by grace
and to the Glory On High!

Painting from Utopia The Paradise of Dreams, from I Will Be Heard Wordpress website.

IMAGINE (8/2/2003)

Imagine a world
free of violence and lust,
full of mutual helping
and true love,
a world whose inhabitants
believe in themselves,
which is to say,
in their own spiritual essence,
and where the myth
of materialism
has been thoroughly dispelled.
Aye! Surely 't would be
such a great world, indeed!
Surely so it would.
Praise God! I say, Praise God!

Image from Destroying Nature is Destroying Life, Campaign by Illusion, Pinterest website.

PARASITE (7/29/1999)

As mankind continues
to over-populate and over-pollute the world,
to graspingly and grubbing-ly
parasite its resources,
to emulate and glorify
his/her own creations,
while ignoring the inherent spirit
in all the Great Rest of Life,
and the wise ecological system
anciently coevolved among
all diverse kinds,
he/she only sets him/herself up
for his/her own worst victim
to become! Surely, truly,
none of this thé
Light of Day shall stand!
Praise God! Amen. Amen.

Photo by author, of Iguazu Falls from Brazilian side at morning. October, 2004.

A SHRINE (7/27/1999)

Consider the world a shrine,
place where so many lifetimes
and so-called "death times,"
cycles of fleshy attachment
and detachment have been lived
by myriad souls so diversely evolved,
yet ever so intrinsically related.
—A holy shrine, I say,
place of suffering and joy,
of growing pains and happy triumphs,
according to the diverse
stages in which one's involved
and all mediated from Heaven on High!

Surely so consider ye
this life, this world: this *school*
… this evolutionary progress,
that is at times a struggle
at other times a graceful flow,
but which always on
to the very highest of goals
does go,
ever by grace
and to the glory
of very God on Highest High!
Praise God! I say, Praise God!
And Hallelujah! shout.

Photo by author from forest with oaks, mossy rocks and decomposing,
leafy soil. Lassen County, California. 11/2012.

ROT—NOT A BAD THING! (7/26/1999)

Thank God for rot and recycling,
that so-called decline,
death and decay
may pave the way
for new and better times arising…
times filled with "old" souls
now made "new,"
for recycling on this Earth,
as, indeed, upon other meant
planes of dwelling.
Thank God then
for the clearers of the way,
even betimes for those
who of necessity subject
themselves to deal in death,
and for all the decomposers
who themselves then in turn
relinquish their hold on the body
and decomposed are,

For these mortal remains
turn and replenish the soil,
as from so-called death
again arises and continues
precious life's renewal.
Truly all this is so wisely
conceived… discovered… experienced… lived!
Praise God!

NEGATIVE REACTIONS (7/22/1999)

Negative attitudes
result in negative reactions!
When the souls of mankind
ruthlessly put down
the Great Rest of Life with whom
they share this planet Earth as home,
they cause horrible negative reactions
against themselves in future times,
that they might learn
true reverence for life
—all in relationship to God!

WORLDLY MONUMENTS (7/19/1999)

There's many an external
monument created
in the name of communication,
but none can compare
with a single inspired moment
experienced by any soul,
nor can any such worldly monument
alone and by itself this command.
Surely not. Praise God! Amen.

MONEY (7/17/1999)

People are conditioned today
from the time they are born
to the time that they die
to believe that money is truth
and worldly possession is reality,
when both alike
are utter lies,
for those who put their faith
and trust and effort
in these end up
empty and depraved,
and finally dead,
dead in spirit, if not in body dead.
—Surely none of this
the Light of Day shall stand!
Praise God! Amen.

WORLDLY SUCCESS (7/17/1999)

There's many a worldly success
rich in material possessions,
so called "high" in society,
yet who's become
a dismal moral failure,
spiritually bankrupt,
for dis-attuned and out of touch, *et cetera.*
So envy not
such as him or her,
for there's so much
more to life than this!
Praise God!

Photo by author of backlit maple leaves, mid-elevation Sierra Nevada western slope.
El Dorado County. 11/2012.

BREATHING, DRINKING, EATING (7/12/1999)

Breathing the air,
we communicate with all the atmosphere!
Drinking water:
with all the lakes, the rivers and the streams,
the clouds and the oceans!
Eating food, we communicate
with all the rocks, soils and sands,
plant and animal bodies.
And through these
means of communication
we are also inspired,
through the all-combining
Living Presence
whose source most Heavenly is!

BEWARE MUNDANE AUTHORITY (7/12/1999)

Learn the art
of staying free
from worldly dictatorships
especially those vicious,
oft cleverly disguised,
mundane authorities
who would seize
hold of your heart and mind and will
through oft subtle and devious ways.
Be pure enough
to slay them with
the Holy Sword of Truth,
brought back to life
within your consciousness
and higher conscience,
by grace of God. Praise God!

Photo by author of South Fork of the American River along U.S. Highway 50, near Kyburz, California. Looking upslope to east. 11/2012.

GEOMANCY (7/12/1999)

Vibrations
of different places or regions
are powerful! There are
special messages in these,
written in the very ethers
of Time. I think here
of ancient Egyptian lands,
of holy Israel, of soaring Andes,
even of my present life's
native land of Nevada,
mystic and austere,
and, so, become
ever so appreciative
of this planet Earth,

all of whose diverse
regions are necessary
to the whole globe,
even as a perfect sphere
unites all of its parts,
each region offering
each unique, yet universal soul
some special lesson,
some unique point of perspective
indispensable for its advancement
as well as an opportunity
to uniquely contribute, according to the time.
Truly so I do.
Praise God! I say, Praise God! Amen.

Full Deck of 52 Playing Cards
Image by pixorama, from creativemarket website.

FULL DECK (2/8/2005)

Life is like
a full deck of cards
in that it takes
all distinctive characters
to make up a world,
and what's more:
a spiritual dimension;
and we each
not only hold,
but *are*
one of these
ever vitally related cards.
Praise God!

THOUGHT, ETHICAL LIFE, GOD

LANGUAGE OF THOUGHT (9/1/2020)

I wish to comment
on that
exquisite subtlety
that one can realize
in one's thoughts
and the universally
connected language of thought…
and to affirm
that all thoughts
are ever linked,
universally intercommunicate…
and that thought
is ever linked to feeling…
though sometimes
it is a question
as to which of these:
thought or feeling,
takes the lead…
or if they are
really ever apart.

Photo from The 14 Most Beautiful Christmas Trees Around the World, from fodors website.

CHRISTMAS POEM (2002)

Lest we forget
Life has many Great Wonders for us yet
in store, as Time ever reveals.
—Have Faith and be of Good Cheer!
God has promised these to us,
each according to its time,
but we must keep our promises to Him,
of a faithful, hoping, truly Loving Heart,
ever striving on,
one Bright with Heavenly visions,
and to these be True and
not sin-given!
Praise God! Amen. Amen.

MY GOD'S BLUE BLISS (a *tetrametric rubaiyat*, 5/26/2001)

I find myself now fifty-two,
a lonely wanderer so blue,
or so 't would seem but for my muse,
one wholly real as me or you!

… My muse in whose most varied moods,
sometimes excited, sometimes soothed,
my heart, my mind, my will bedight,
according to some Higher Truths!

Now speech and music, image, sound,
within my conscious life resound!
—Oh! Lord! Now how my spirit soars
in conscious these to come full round!

… Time's coalescing puzzle this,
no piece of which I'd ever miss,
for I behold with future sight,
Solution Full—my God's Blue Bliss!

TO PLUCK A THOUGHT—AN *ORVILLETTE* (1/30/2003)

… To pluck a thought out of thin air,
to plumb a feeling deep within:
of what avail I ask you now?
'T is soul's fine work, one, Oh! so Fair!

To pluck a thought out of thin air,
to soar to heights, defy the world,
—by means deemed strange—don't ask me how!
'T is soul's fine work, one, Oh! so Pearled!

… To pluck a thought out of thin air
unravels myst'ries so profound, such
phases one with a great Pow!
'T is soul's fine work, one, Oh! so Crowned!

To pluck a thought out of thin air
brings one to face oneself as well.
—Can you not see?! 'T is Plan Divine!
'T is soul's fine work, one, Oh! so Belle!

TEMPTATION (7/11/1995)

The easy, tempting way of vice
becomes a slippery road to Hell,
as the more one moves along,
the faster one descends
… as many a poor soul should attest!

EXAMPLE (3/14/2001)

Be an uplifted,
inspired example yourself,
oh! my soul, of
all the great, positive,
virtuous affirmation
in and for life,
for, thus, your own
true living example
shall positively effectuate,
gloriously dramatic change
throughout, for beyond, the world.
Praise God!

GOD: RESTORER OF THE DOWN-FALLEN (1998)

After one's choices for sin
have made a ruin
of one's current cycle, or life,
God picks up the pieces thereof
and puts them back together again.
And for this reason
we justly call our
ever living, ever loving God:
the Very Greatest of All,
the Supreme, the Most High,
the One who never fell
and, so, who never fails,
the Most Worthy of Our Love,
the Most Faithful and True
—and so must we be to Thee!

ADVANCEMENT (9/1/1999)

No true advancement
is ever made by putting others down,
though it appears this way
to the worldly point of view,
for, rather,
all the very opposite is true!
Advancement is made
by lifting others up,
sincerely and out of
worldly disinterested
love for this fellow self,
and because one perceives
the special Divine within
each special soul embarked upon
its special way… and then
in this brave act
of virtuous giving, relating,
one oneself uplifted is
… though all love is
true giving alone
for love's sake alone,
and, by the same token,
a loving in receiving
another's true love for one.
Praise God! Amen. Amen.

REPROOF (8/26/1999)

Time is vast;
and there is ever the reproof
for every rash,
worldly excess
and overblown claim,
as each and every soul
shall surely come to learn.
Praise God! Amen. Amen.

GODLY SPIRIT (8/24/1999)

Those who speak of
the mystical reality of life and world,
speak of that which
beyond mere tangibles is.
They speak of the Holy Essence,
the Godly Spirit,
that which is known within
and corresponds to
the *withinness* of all things
—the Heaven within—
the finding of oneself in all,
the right reading of all symbols,
the inner reviving!
This pursuit the piercing of
the veil of worldly delusion is.

It is the true
Road to Salvation!
But to get on this
holy road one must
be willing to make sacrifice
of all worldly delusion
and sinful attachment.
This is the noble way.
But each one of us must
decide for him/her/it-self.
Praise God!
… So be unbound by mortal views!
Rise, oh! my soul, to highest heights,
there, life's Eternal panorama to behold
—so beautiful, so joyous, so full of Love!

VISION (10/7/1999)

The experience of life
can be heart-rendering at times,
but ever it is my vision of God
that keeps me going on.
Truly so it does.
Praise God! Amen. Amen.

NOT IN VAIN (8/18/1999)

Know this, oh! my soul:
your soul life
is not in vain!
So, just take care
not to become
hung up on
worldly false values,
so that you may
learn to value
the inner life you lead
and that stores up
such great treasures from Heaven,
which is to say, from God
… unique treasures upon which
all the world depends,
as upon your discovery of them
— then learn to appreciate
the same in everyone,
even those seemingly
most different from yourself.
Surely so do.
Praise God! I say, Praise God!
And Hallelujah! shout.

LOVE

THE GOAL: A POEM ABOUT LOVE (1/24/2001)

Beware of where you place your **heart**
that disillusion yours be **not**,
this bitter fruit you reap to **death**
because of worldly fetish—No!
But keep your heart so fixed upon
that ***Bright Star*** that does still to dawn
that **Star** which, though so far unreached,
yet still touches us with its Light!
In it you well find a sure *guide,*
that in its steadfast **glow** your *quest*
shall ever draw ye *nigh to God,*
for this Light is His own True Love
—our true and perfect **Goal Above!**
Praise God! I say, Praise God! Praise God!

A MAN AND A WOMAN—a *Kelly* (10/30/2000)

A man and a woman
attracted, no one can
divide, part asunder,
when married they're "made one"
so far as this world-hemmed,
long life is concerned!
… Yet those of a higher,
more subtle, fine knowledge
in Love see more than
mere mortals attached.

Photo from Visit The White Cliffs of Dover, England, from audleytravel website.

THE SEA BECKONS (an exercise in identifying with the opposite sex, 5/15/2002)

"Widow Maker"
some call the Sea,
but bristly brine
and salty spume
and blue horizons,
vast and far,
remind me of
my precious Love
and shall so long
as I'll reside
beside these lovely,
deathly waves -
Alas!—that stole
my Love away!
Yet these give life
as well in me:
so much in them
I see, perceive,
for my Beloved's
presence here
to me does sing,
is seen and smelled
and tasted Still—
exquis't'ly felt!—
in salty brine
and fresh, sea air,
in Images
conjured up
from dashing surf—
BENEATH!—
and dreamy clouds—
OVERHEAD!—
as in ALL this
Land-Sea-Sky Match!
… And in the very
stone cliffs His Face is wrought!
… And in these very
rhythmic waves
there is a Pounding of
my Heart's own Song,
commingled with One
now sailed Beyond—
where, too, I'll soon be bound!
Praise God! Amen.

LOVE (3/3/2001)

The experience of Love,
in this life and world,
a Taste of Heaven
most surely is—
this pure spiritual
communication of unity
and caring,
no matter how great
the difference between/among
our creature forms
or worldly situations,
for a Higher Relation
most truly this is,
ever by grace
and to the Glory of God!

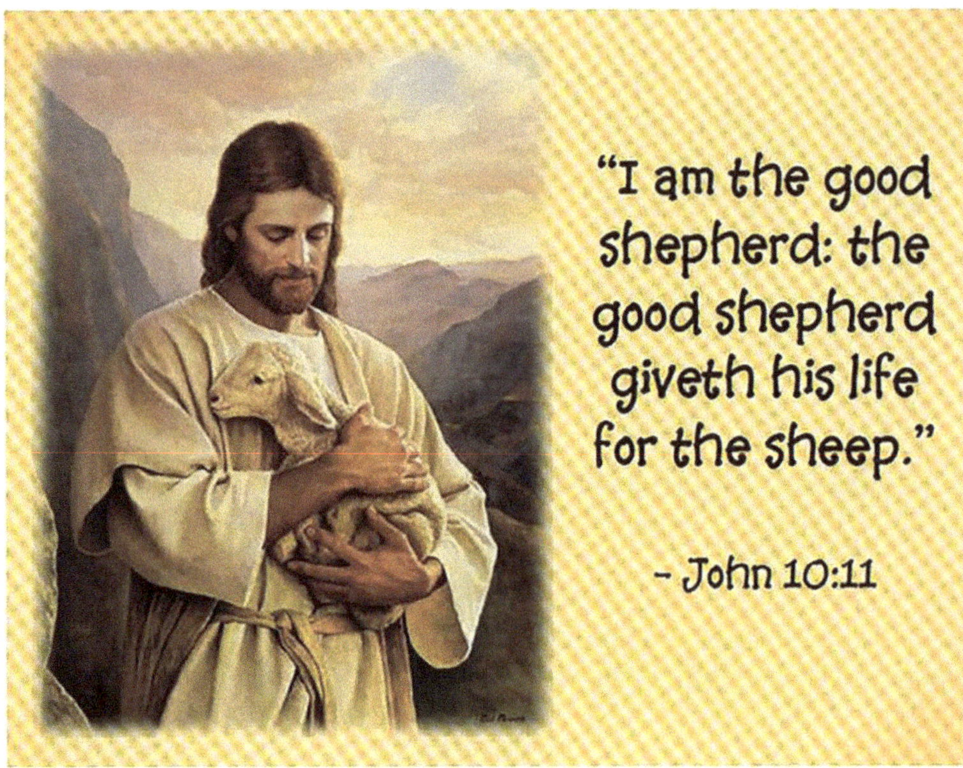

Image from clipart of Jesus Christ as a shepherd, from clipground website.

THE LAMB OF LOVE—AN ONDA MEL (4/20/2001)

Gentle lamb, cradled in Christ's arms,
Adoringly;
Confidingly,
—Surely, you will come to no harm!
Bright spirit uniquely shining,
Conceived Above,
*Pure child of **Love**—*
You're MORE than all world's defining!

… A LOVE (9/1/1999)

There is a love
that goes deep
into the very roots
of our shared relation,
to that time
before the Fall,
before the taint
of sin and false idol
had blotted out
the holy consciousness
of that greatest
and all-uniting
most whole and perfect,
and, now, most restoring
Love of God!

HAPPY… SAD (7/15/2003)

Sad, one becomes happy.
Happy, one grows sad again,
et cetera, et cetera, according
to the great eternal rhythm,
the sweeping melody
that carries one forth,
and all with one,
and one with all,
for ever so mysteriously
we related are.
Truly so. Praise God!

LOVE (7/22/1999)

Love is a wonderful phenomenon:
to experience it is to know
the very spiritual essence of life
and through this one's relationship to ALL.
Truly it is so. Praise God!

Image from 136+ EXCLUSIVE Light Quotes To Brighten Up Your Journey, from bayart website.

THE LIGHT (7/15/1999)

The Light shineth *within*
and therefrom
shall not extinguished be!
It shines in each and every
individual soul,
in every heart and mind and will
and shall not be overcome

by the Darkness,
but shineth still;
no matter what has happened
—*it will forevermore!*
Truly so it shall.
Praise God! Shout Hallelujah!

DARKNESS? (10/18/2003)

Darkness, oh! my soul,
is but the harbinger of Light;
and, so, it is
with every seeming absence, or lack,
for these, keenly felt,
do usher in
the very Fullness and Love
of we all for each other,
for of God!

FACT OF LIFE (2/9/2005)

The karma of loving attachment
is reflected in worldly life, or incarnations,
and our relations therein.
Forming attachment to a woman or man,
as the case may be,
is not as superficial
as many like to believe,
but carries on
in future lifetimes,
when one becomes
the son or daughter,
the mother or father,
of one's former lover.
And there is such great beauty
and wisdom and justice
in this higher
fact of life!
—And plenty of time for this!
Praise God!

TRUTH, UNIVERSAL PRINCIPLES, DIMENSIONS

THE TRUTH (2/7/1999)

The truth abides
and no lie can effectively deny it!
Heavenly is the truth
all in relationship to God!

OMNIPRESENCE (7/27/1999)

The spiritually aware
perceive the Spirit everywhere
and in all Time.
They know all life's
forms, animations,
perceiving in each unique style
a special spiritual state
and condition. This is
the art of perceiving life
that far transcends
the mere science
of superficial measuring
and describing such.
And all our conscious
journey of discovery
full of such art is.
Praise God!

Photo by author from Three Fingers Wild Horse HMA, along lower
Owyhee Reservoir, southeastern Oregon. October 11, 2016.

THE THREE DIMENSIONS (8/2/1999)

It is imperative
that we not only recognize
the various dimensions,
but also rightly prioritize
them unto the highest,
the most all-inclusive
wherein lies
life's greatest, purest truth!
To wit: *Space* that is included
and transcended by *Time;*
Time that is included
and transcended by *Spirit.*
For, in final analysis, it is *Spirit*
that is all life's greatest truth,
and, so, all the world's,
and World of worlds,
for *Spirit* very Godly is!

Photo by author of two deer near Iron Gate Reservoir, south side, northern California. Spring, 2019.

PARALLEL (7/27/1999)

There is between
one's thoughts and feelings
and their progress toward truth
many a wondrous parallel
in the externally manifest world.
This relation is one of
cause and effect.
And this can work both ways
when specially imbued
becomes these effects.
Praise God!

ACTION: REACTION (7/22/1999)

"For every action,
there is an equal
but opposite reaction"
applies as much to
inner-personal relations
as to inter-species relations —
that we all together come
to truly Love One Another
through our common
worship—and each our unique glorification - of God -
our most precious Lord God
whom we all share.
Praise God! Forever and ever.

FORMS (10/2003)

Forms are wondrous:
to see how they incorporate
all things into one
great design.
And so are all our lives:
these all relate,
connect to one another.
And as each one
purifies his/her
outlook on life,
so he/she begins
again to discern
the interconnecting lines,
the patterns and the forms, *et cetera*.
And the unifying plan, or design,
with its ever life-saving
meaning is brought home.
Truly so it is. Praise God! Amen. Amen.

SHARING (7/17/1999)

What do we all share
if not Time?!
And if we all share Time,
we all share Space as well.
But most of all
it is *Spirit*
that we all share,
for Spirit unites us…
beautiful, transcendent Spirit
that all Time
and, so, all Space
includeth and surpasseth.
Truly so it doeth.
Praise God!

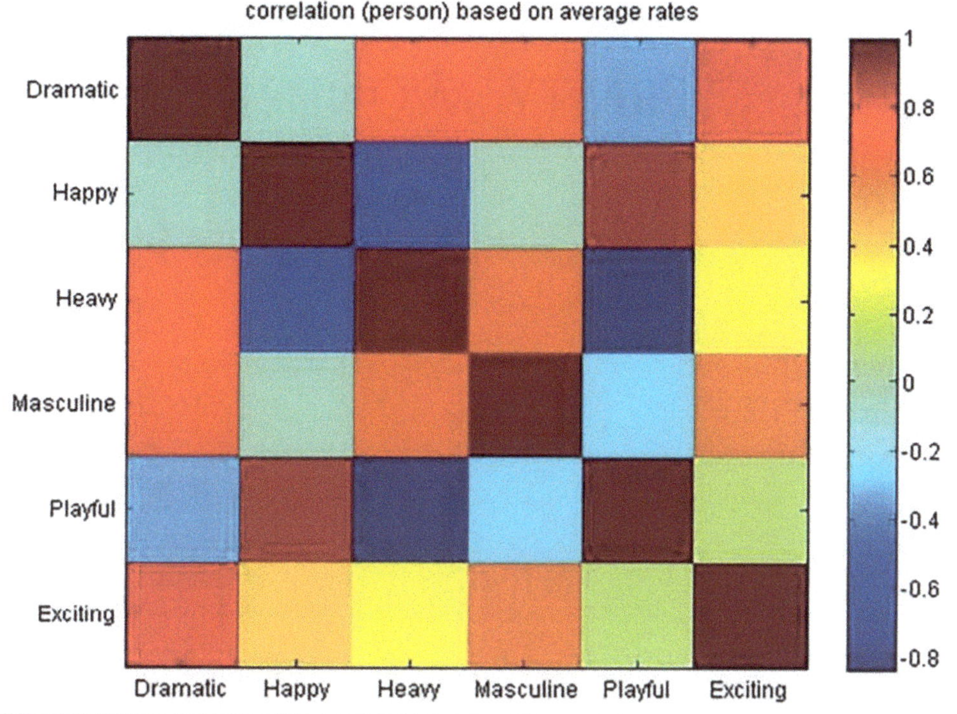

Image from BBC-Research and Development, Musical Moods, from BBC website.

SPIRITUAL MATRIX (7/15/1999)

As spirits
we all together form
the spiritual matrix,
or context, for
each other's actions
in spirit,
which is to say,
in quintessential thought, word, and deed.
And no individual spirit
is without its
special universal effect.
Truly so. Praise God! And Hallelujah! shout.

ETERNITY, WONDER

ETERNAL SOUL (8/7/1999)

Each soul goes on forever;
ever has been, ever is, and ever will be
one with all Eternal Truth.
And in this process called "living"
is Truth's rediscovery,
as forth out of Darkness
and unto Light one emerges,
back from the Fall
and unto God!
… Believe in this, oh! my soul,
whoever you are,
and you will be saved,
by the everlasting grace
and to the everlasting glory
of the Lord our most precious
God On High!

WONDER (7/31/1999)

To grasp the wonder
of just one moment in Time
is to glimpse all Eternity,
in essence. So look
with heartfelt welcome
upon where you are
right here and now,
if you would appreciate life,
for lest you so learn
you will not appreciate
any of it.

WONDERFUL (7/18/1999)

Wonderful how
all our lives
ever related are,
for all our beings
from the same Source come!
To realize this
is such great liberation
from artificial barriers imposed,
from worldly lies
unto God's Heavenly Truth.
Praise God!

Painting from Celebrating Indigenous Peoples Day, from 3 chicspolitico website.

BEAUTY: A CHANT (7/12/1999)

Beauty there is in death,
beauty there is in birth,
because these miracles tell
of the soul's passage in and out
of incarnate life
and force us
to consider life's
higher meanings, its relation
to Eternal Truth,
to God.
Beauty there is in death!
Beauty there is in life!

MORALITY, ETHICS, JUSTICE, GOOD AND EVIL, VIRTUE

Painting from Indian war chant, from YouTube — lakotachevalfou.

VANQUISHING EVIL (8/7/1999)

Against seemingly impossible odds,
and when least expected by worldly smug
vain types, you shall
vanquish over all sin and evil,
all worldly darkness and lies,
by your very uplifted thoughts and feelings
and willings to the Most High!
And your home shall become
a most mighty sanctuary,
unassailable by the forces of wickedness,
however these may surround…
a home invincible in the good,
for a Heavenly channel,
pure and uplifted

in and by God's pure
and perfect truth.
While all profaned lives around
shall go down into the devouring
flames of Hell, you shall
stand, oh! pure and valiant soul,
and where none have stood
since before the Fall;
and not just stand,
but further advance ye shall
unto God's ever beautiful and true,
Light of Salvation and Life and Love.

RIGHTEOUS (7/30/1999)

A righteous life
is an unassailable fortress
that shall withstand
ALL the vicissitudes,
the tides and winds
of Time. Praise God! Amen.

HUBRIS (7/31/2003)

Let not worldly hubris
wax in your heart
and mind and will,
for it is an obscurer of such
and ever is cut
to the quick
by Time and Fate
and Sacred Justice!
Truly so it is.
Praise God!

Painting from Saint Francis of Assisi, His Life in Art, from Riverdale Press website.

THE SAINT (7/28/1999)

Few people appreciate
the role of the saint
in society today.
Yet it is verily
the highest of roles, as by
maintaining the conscious link
with Heaven such proves
a veritable life-saver
for all concerned.
And we are all related,

and for this reason
when the saint ascends
to higher conscious planes,
ones closer to God,
so all the world
likewise ascends,
for thoughts and feelings
have universally uplifting wings.
Truly so they do!
Praise God! And Hallelujah! shout.

VIRTUE (7/27/1999)

He who
consciously possesses virtue
possesses more than
all worldly wealth!
He who
knows peace of mind
and Heavenly order
together with purity of heart
and nobility of enterprise,
or will,
has reached the objective
of all this worldly school.
Truly so he has.
Praise God! I say, Praise God!

PETTINESS (7/22/1999)

Pettiness is the enemy
of all noble, virtuous advancement,
the "friend" of sin,
but sin ever proves
itself to be
no one's true friend
at all, indeed!

Illustration from Woman generous clipart, clipart collection — Clipart's World 2019 website.

GIVING… RECEIVING (8/18/1999)

Higher metaphysical law
teaches us that
in giving we receive,
hence the beautiful consequence
of generosity…
though we must give
out of love for the other,
out of identification therewith,
all in relationship to God.
Praise God!

CORRUPTION (7/17/1999)

A "big head"
often corresponds
to a small and petty mind;
a vain and worldly self-vaunting
heart and will,
with all the abysmal
corruption thereof!
Surely, truly,
none of this thé
Light of Day shall stand!
Praise God! Amen.

DECEIT (7/15/1999)

Be not suckered in
by worldly enticements,
promises of paradise and joy
centered around earthly
possessions of the flesh
and the mere physical
realm of bodies and processes
taken in and of themselves,
and including the mundanely intellectual
knowledge thereof,
for what an utter lie these ever prove,
so terribly disillusioning
—what a horrible self-deceit!
Be not so deluded and deceived,
but, rather, look to all of life's
True and Heavenly Source
—all its great, transcendent Spirit
in whole and perfect
relationship to God! Praise God!

Image from Compassion Horses, Animals, Animal Posters, Pininterest website.

COMPASSION (7/13/1999)

Compassion
the very crown
of wisdom is,
the real proof
that one has
finally made the grade,
attained enlightenment,
risen free
from petty worldly attachment,
possessiveness, jealousy, greed,
lust, false worldly values,
and all the other
ponderous weights
that hold any soul down!

LOVE OF JUSTICE (7/14/1999)

Who loves justice
more than worldly life itself?
Who gives the righteous
joyful welcome?
The lovers of
higher spiritual truth!
The reverers of life!
Such prove their mettle true
by standing up for what is good,
making all needed
worldly self-sacrifice.
Such will be welcomed
to their great
and sweet reward
in Heaven,
to receive a "well-done"
from God
after the final curtain descends
upon this their relatively brief
and fleeting worldly life.
Truly so they shall.
Praise God! And Hallelujah! shout.

THE GOOD FIGHT (8/28/2020)

BE THE LIGHT!
RISE UP—FIGHT
THE GOOD FIGHT!

LIFE'S HEAVENLY IDEAL, GOAL, PEACE

Image from Shining Star of Bethlehem — Stock Vector,
copyright fogbird #4174328, from Depositphotos website.

THE GUIDING STAR (7/31/1999)

He who retains
the great overview of life,
relating this
one mortal experience with
all past and all future,
keeps on an even keel,
is not "taken in,"
keeps sight through insight upon
life's great and noble ideal
by which to guide him/herself,
as a ship's navigator
by some sure Star
—that surely shall not fail!
Truly it shall not.
Praise God! I say, Praise God!
And Hallelujah! shout.

INNER PEACE (7/27/1999)

Be at peace with your inner self,
weaned from external distraction,
harmonious within, feeling
full and happy and content
in that blessed stillness
which is your Heavenly inheritance
and everlasting place of refuge,
which nothing and no one
merely worldly can
take away from you,
for this is your
own special branch of Heaven
that like any branch of any tree
to all other branches
as to the main trunks
and the Trunk
connected is.
… And it is in
both the give and the take
that one knows and feels
oneself not to be just a part
but the whole of all that is!
All in everlasting
relationship to God!

HEAVENLY GIFTS (7/14/1999)

Never become
so caught up in
worldly affairs
and preoccupations
that you spare no time
to stop and think,
meditate and reflect,
to know what's really
going on in life,
to clear away
the worldly confusion,
to receive
the Heavenly perspective,
consoling insight,
inspired directive.
Praise God! Praise God!

PERFECTION (7/12/1999)

The spirit of life,
seeing, hearing:
in all ways sensing
imperfection,
sets about to restore
perfection
from that sublime
and inner sense,
or image innate, or voice
that, or, rather, *who*
Divine must surely is!

LIFE'S PAIN AND JOY—FIVE *CINQUAINS* (4/12/2004)

Headache,
dull, depressing,
makes me seek God's blessing,
and no more to take for granted
Virtue.

Wonder:
life forever
unfolds within each one.
There is no gain without some pain.
—How true!

Joyful!
The sun does rise
again to greet new day.
Another chance is given now.
—Thank God!

Who knows
what day will bring?
some unique unveiling
for each one of us salvation:
Lesson.

A Goal
an inner light
reveals. Ancient promise
just now fulfilled, yet still points on
to God!

Photo by author, showing overgrazed lands with large white bull on BLM lands leased for cattle grazing, south of Mountain Home, Idaho. Ca. 2004.

OVERGRAZING RECTIFIED BY GRACE—A *BALANCE* POEM (3/26/2004)

I find it most remarkable how man
o'erlooks the crux of major wrong!
Take overgrazing Earth
by hordes of cows
so forced,
coerced!
I ask just now
how can there be such dearth
of conscience, rev'rence pure and strong!
But it's my knowledge sure that we now can
face up to past mistakes and take a stand,
make bold our steps for change and long
to reestablish mirth
by sweat of brow,
remorse
—no curse,
but blessing!—how
among all kinds we forth
relating harmony will throng
the very gates of Heav'n—Bright Future Land!

REDEMPTION—A *LAI* POEM (2/2005)

A bright new lesson
for each life session
must come…
just compensation
for tribulation
which from
right's brave adoption
came as condition
—saved Mum!

TRUST, BELIEF, FAITH

TRUST (7/31/1999)

Those who put their
trust in the world
shall taste death,
but those who believe
in God's Heavenly Truth
concerning *ALL*,
even this manifest
life and world,
shall uplifted be.
Truly so they shall.
Praise God!
Hallelujah!

A quest for longevity. Five hundred years ago, the Spanish explorer Ponce de León drank his way around the Florida coast during his expedition to find the legendary fountain of youth.

Painting from AgeingUniverse-review website.

FOUNTAIN OF YOUTH (7/20/1999)

Look forward
with uplifted belief
to the future,
for this is
the secret of youth.
Praise God!

PATIENCE (7/18/1999)

Those who bide their time patiently,
seeking to do God's will,
answering the Heavenly
calling for their life,
not seeking to rashly impose
a worldly corrupted will,
shall find themselves
most blessed
—and oft when least expected!
Truly so they shall.
Praise God! And shout Hallelujah!

Photo by author, of lovely lilacs in blossom early spring, 2006.

WHEN IT COMES TO NATURE: OPEN YOUR HEART AND LET THE LIGHT SHINE OUT AND IN! (a *Paean* of Belief in Life on Earth, 8/30/2020 & revised through 10/5/2020)

Consider in the World of Nature,
that which or, rather, *who* is born,
made manifest here in this incarnate plane!

Consider all the various
and vastly numbered
plants and animals,
decomposers, large and small,
and all the creatures
that make life possible,
that make us function as a whole!

Consider vast skies overhead,
protective magnetic fields,
magnificently colored *aurora borealis*,
deep, blue oceans,
gleaming lakes, so pure and clean;
rushing streams that seem
never-ending, bright, cheering,

as they wend their way
down from god-like peaks
to ultimate lakes, subterranean
basins or even vast, deep oceans,
there to circulate nutrients
then evaporate and return again.

Consider the world of soils,
so rich in texture,
minerals, moisture,
teaming minute
organisms, *et cetera.*
These sustain us all,
for without such
where would life be?

Yes, consider all sorts
of Nature's scenes,
for their very thought
purifies, refreshes—
puts us *in tune*!
And these diverse, yet
interrelated, components
themselves do balance out,
inter-complement and, thus, sustain
all us Earth-dwellers, or Earthlings.

Internalize this great marvel!
Identify with it, if you can.
For such marvelous intricacy
should not be
taken for granted.
And we in human form
owe such an enormous
debt of gratitude to this!
For all who dwell here
in whatever form, place or time
ever interrelate, interlock together
in a liberating, evolving—

ultimately most progressive way!
And this I affirm—most fervently!

And so, again, I say:
Take care to *internalize*
all the greater, higher,
unifying truth concerning Life!
Regard not other species
as mere externalities
to be done with as you please!
For each in its own special way
indispensably relates to thee—to all!
And with each succeeding moment
a further liberating truth
has been, is and will be
ours to discover!

So, when you venture
into the World of Nature,
be this some mighty forest,
vast ocean, mountain high
or valley low, sere desert plain,
mysterious, descending cavern,
or awesome, replete-with-life bushland—
there and to this be sure to display a bright shining
attitude, openness and true caring!
Do uplifted believing in
and enlightened identification with
all those who surround you.
For this shall cause
all your fellow beings—
regardless superficial differences
to respond in corresponding,
welcoming, sharing—
even loving tune!

For the natural world about us,
into which we have been born,
holds such amazing lessons!...

lessons tracing back
to Life's Very Source!

Fellow soul, fellow sentient being
whoever you are, ever strive to
greet all the wonderful
presences about you
with a positive, faithful, believing,
highest-truth-upholding, *caring—*
most of all a charitable, truly loving
attitude,
born of higher mind's
conception and attunement
that opens up the heart
and in unison
the sacred will
to realize with all these
Beneficent Cooperation
—no matter how distinct
in form or mode of living
your neighbor seems!
Let there be a
Positive Recognition…
a Mutual Co-affirming,
for all else death is!

No longer target
those of "other" species
as the enemy to be ground
up by a selfish, indifferent,
uncharitable and even hostile
attitude, as though
they were mere "things"
to control and manipulate,
use up and then destroy,
for such a negative attitude
will only, most of all,
boomerang upon yourself!

For as realized the *Ancient Mariner*
in Coleridge' famous rime:
He prayeth well, who loveth well
Both man and bird and beast.
He prayeth best, who loveth best
All things both great and small.
And let us add:
All creatures within themselves
most sacredly imbued
with higher purpose are…
possess a holy goal
toward which both they
and we do roll…
toward which all kinds—
all beings tend,
as we so perfectly
interweave and wend
our unfolding,
ever so simultaneously
consciously awakening
Beingnesses through Time.

And as to the essence of each fellow creature
and one's own inherently recognized essence,
one will ever
find these are the same
and that they reside forever
in that most cherished
all-uniting
upon-all-shining
and all-revealing
Spirit Divine!
Praise God! Amen.

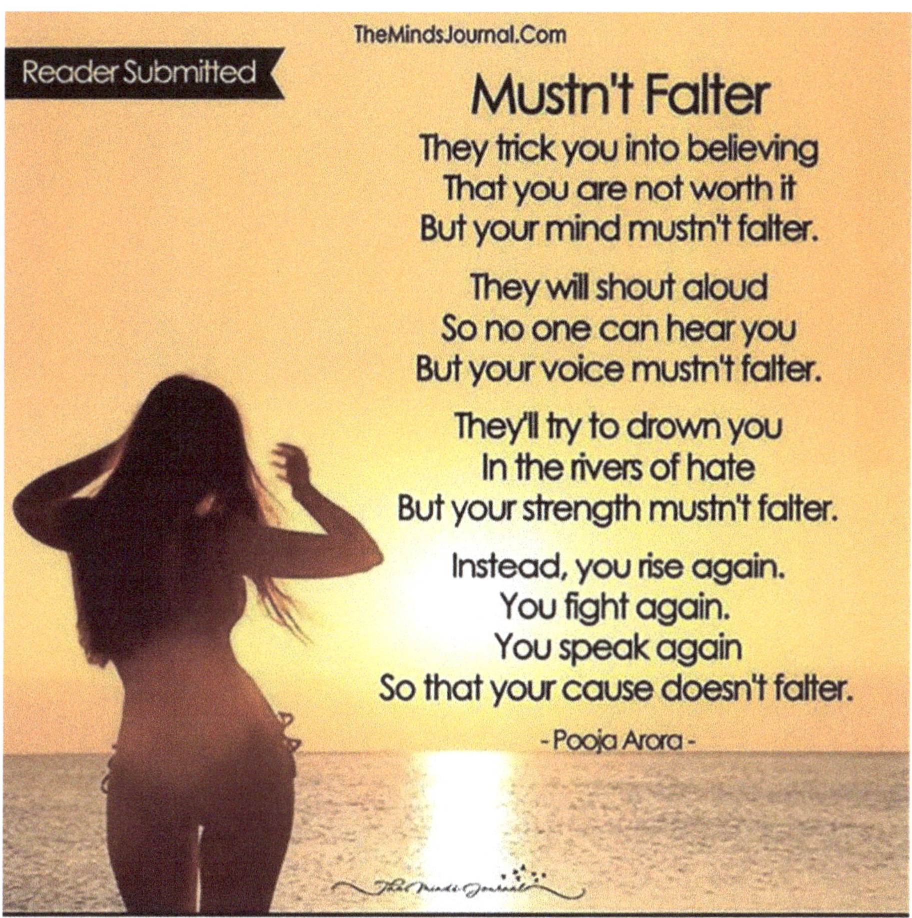

Image from TheMindsJournal.Com. Pooja Arora poem and photo possibly. Reader Submitted.

REINCARNATION

Passages from "Do Animals Reincarnate?" article in *Reincarnation Report* (10/1982) by Craig C. Downer.

Evidence for reincarnation among humans is more tangible than among animals because of man's ability to communicate his experiences through language. Through related experiences contained in dreams, extra-sensory perception, astral projection and hypnosis, a great volume of evidence has been amassed in support of human reincarnation. However, the distinct possibility and overwhelming likelihood exists that if reincarnation pertains to man, it pertains to the other individual life forms which share in the cycle of life and death on Earth. Although people cannot generally speak and listen to animals and plants, there is much about our fellow creatures which speaks for itself for reincarnation. Take instinct, for example. Most species appear to possess an ancestral memory. Biologists call this "genetic inheritance," but on a spiritual level, "genetic inheritance" could be nothing less than the memory and acquired ability of past lives. Strong support for ancestral memory and a spiritual aspect to life's evolution can be gained by considering the following:

Golden Plover young are known to migrate over a complicated course of several thousand miles, from the Arctic tundra to the Gran Chaco of central South America. Lacking the guidance of adults, who leave before their nestlings have perfected their flying ability, these young plovers are able to fly the precise migratory pathways of their ancestors. This pathway includes specific ponds and marshes utilized by the species for thousands of years.

Many species of migratory birds, particularly ducks, are innately equipped with stellar charts, mentally present, and are able to migrate across oceans and continents according to navigational "flight plans." When clouds obscure the heavens, these migratory birds often lose their way or take cover until they can again see their way clearly. It is known that the abilities of these birds are innate, for they migrate "first time" without the guidance of adults.

Nest building activity in many avian species is inborn. After four generations of removal from nesting materials, African Weaver birds are able to construct their own species-specific nests…. They are untaught and entirely guided by instinct. Such instinct could well be the memory of nest building acquired over many past lives.

The spawning migrations of freshwater eels take them from the coastal rivers of Europe and North America to their natal waters in the Sargasso Sea. In the Sargasso Sea, they complete their life cycle giving rise to "leptocephali." Over the course of a few years, these baby eels then migrate to the same rivers in Europe and North America from which their forebears came. Their return cannot be simply explained by random coincidence, for the offspring return to the identical rivers their progenitors originally left. Each population has its "home" river. A similar migratory pattern occurs in several salmon species and steelhead trout.

From a *reincarnationist* [term used by this magazine] point of view, such migrations point to the remembrance among individual fish of certain environmental clues, be they chemicals in the waters of their native streams or the patterns and kinesthetics of ocean currents, including temperature, velocity and direction. Experiencing these environmental patterns repeatedly and over many lifetimes leads to an innate pattern of migration….

From the point of view of the individual's evolution, and bearing reincarnation in mind, the acquisition of physical and behavioral traits through the experience gained during Earth Lives may not appear so unreasonable. Could we behold the entire breadth and scope of life's reality, I believe we would find that life's progress through time does reflect a spiritual, or inner, evolution, both of the individual and of groups of individuals united to varying degrees by common or shared experience. It is well to avoid being overwhelmed by superficial data. To gain real insight into life's course, one must use the imagination—as well as the intuition—and consider first the inner, or spiritual, reality and second the outer, or material, reality as a reflection of the former….

Biologists attribute embryonic development to the programming present in the genetic material, or DNA strands. And it is certain that a very subtle and complex genetic mechanism exists. But to say that this chemical process is the entire explanation is simplistic in the extreme. There is much in man's embryological recapitulations of protozoans, jellyfish, gill-bearing fish, reptiles, and apes and the embryonic recapitulation of other species to suggest a corresponding psychic recapitulation. Perhaps the individual psyche "relives" his past experiential evolution, corresponding to millions of years of life on Earth, and this psychic reliving [in accelerated manner known to the spirit] is then materially reflected in the embryonic development of the individual.

The observation that in-utero development recapitulates past evolution points to a profound psychic process. What I am referring to is a "spiritual evolution" that is a compounding, ever-augmenting and progressive expansion and perfection of the individual soul. Basically, this process is an "unfolding," as the Latin origin of the word "e-volve" suggests. For all that one is and all that one is to become is latent within. The environment life inhabits—the earth, the sky, and the ocean—is the medium of our evolution, but not the cause. It may appear that the obstacles to our physical survival dictate our evolution, but the true cause of life's progression is inner, or spiritual in nature, no matter whether we speak of humans or of fish, of plants or of animals, of complex life forms or of simple life forms. For life is, in essence, spiritual: self-aware and self-directed. All that is manifested outwardly proceeds first from within. [For this article, I received high praise from the editor of this magazine, as from readers too.]

Excerpts from "The Spiritual Evolution: A Book on Reincarnation and Evolution" (1981) by author.

Prologue

The concepts of reincarnation and the evolution of life are so akin that an ideological union is not hard to conceive, especially when there is a world full of evidence to support this marriage.

Considering all the vast volumes of soul-experience in all the lives ever lived in whatever species or places or times, something tells me that there is a spiritual, as well as a physical, building or evolution—and, furthermore, that this spiritual evolution is reflected perfectly in the physical. Some predetermined bent arising from my inmost being tells me that my very awareness and existence do not simply vanish at death. The "I am" is conserved and is united with a universal "I am" that is inherent in every life from virus, ameba, plant, and animal to man himself. By becoming more aware of this, we can greatly improve our lives.

And I do truly believe that in simply becoming aware of "what is," we do cause even much greater things to be. In this belief I have written this book, hoping it can help you tap the treasures of your spirit and manifest them to the world.

For I hold that the same evolution which occurs in your present life occurs throughout your many, many lives since the very beginning. It is your experiences and insights which shape the attitudes and abilities you express. And this is how you have evolved spiritually, just as you evolve in this life from moment to moment. Indeed, the evolution of all life forms is a living, experiencing, and growing process of vast scale which is reflected perfectly in all physical manifestations from the body to everything you touch in some way.

Call upon your inner sense of self-pride and recall your vast age and experience. Try to imagine it. Then, come with me as we embark upon this marvelous contemplation of the vast spiritual evolution which has blossomed forth, like a spreading, magnanimous, old tree, into all the diverse individuals and species that have existed and do exist in our world. As I attempt to make cogent the spiritual, reincarnative process of evolution, imagine yourself evolving through a vast array of experiences that fashion your abilities, conceptions, and bodily manifestations in a continuous unfoldment. Identify with the various forms of life—even plants, if you can. Stretch your mind to conceive beyond what you are already capable of conceiving. Put forth effort and you will experience a greater satisfaction than ever you could by a mere falling back into old trains of thought . . .

Virgin Cloud Forest from Purshi Valley, Sangay National Park – All photos © Craig C. Downer

Chapter 1

Reincarnation

Is Spirit conserved just as matter and energy are? To this question I answer an emphatic *yes* while pointing my finger at Reincarnation for my justification.

Reincarnation is quite obvious in this world of ours to anyone who can see the river which flows in myriad trickles throughout the ages. This river is, indeed, composed of the same water in one century as in the following and in the preceding centuries. It is the water of spirits flowing from the beginning to the end of this seeming eternity of the universe's progression through the ages—through the whole of space-time. These spirits are all the creatures that have ever lived. And each one of them has occupied myriad lives since the original Fall from Perfection. The Preacher has summed it up beautifully when he says: "All the rivers run into the sea; yet the sea is not full; unto the place from whence the rivers come, thither they return again" (Eccl. 1:7, King James Version).

Reincarnation is evinced in all the observations of life when one accepts life's basic immortal nature. Instinct is memory, not just some queer chemical blueprint in the chemical coding of life. And even though, in the genetic material, there is a manifestation of the experiences of the ancestors, this is no cause of instincts in the newborn. Rather, the experience of living and of learning causes the material imprints in the genetic mechanisms and directs the genetic manifestation of the individual at conception and throughout embryonic development.…

I have noticed an inexplicable recognition with some people whom I meet for the first time in this life. And often a tidal wave of feelings, or vibrations, hits me upon meeting a person like this. This person, no doubt, triggers the subconscious memory of all my experience around him/her in a past life or in past lives. And it wells up mutedly to my conscious in a nonspecific but strongly tangible and definite, feeling, or vibration. This, also, occurs with places, buildings, musical pieces, songs, and languages, and nearly everything to some extent. This feeling of *deja-vu* is really quite common, and I doubt that anyone could honestly say that he has never experienced it. It may be that he never gave it any serious consideration when he did experience it, as he was so caught up in his present life. Perhaps, the attraction to the opposite sex, and particularly to certain types of the opposite sex, is a *deja-vu* experience of high intensity, involving all one's past mates. Also, one's natural affinities for certain lands, cultures, and peoples could indicate past lives.

When I traveled through Turkey, I experienced the most uncanny recognition and wonder when passing Mount Ararat. This is the highest mountain in Turkey at 16,945 feet. It lies near the eastern border with Iran. I had passed it before on my way to India, but it was upon my return that I felt this feeling of *deja-vu.* It was as though part of my very identity was connected to this looming, majestic mountain, whose snowy covering, standing out against the barren plain and icy sky, gave it a very hoary aspect. It was pure magic, for my very being extended out to include the mountain and the ethos of its inhabitants and those of the plain around. Part of my identity must have been formed in and around this holy mountain in a past life or in past lives; for how else can I explain the vast feelings and associations which came welling up as from a bygone time upon my witnessing the mountain? Feelings which seemed to contain within themselves the genius of whole cultures and long eras, of whole civilizations and the silent, unrecorded histories of many lives, drudgeries, hopes, and aspirations—all these came to me. It was, indeed, a magical experience. How can I convey it? To appreciate it one must have experienced an equivalent. But there are other types of *deja-vu* which the reader might more readily recall in his experience.

I notice that sometimes I write and use words I am entirely unfamiliar with. When I am searching for a way to express something, these words well up from my subconscious, and I find them the exact expression of my feeling or idea. And I mysteriously know their precise definitions. Even as a young boy I remember that words would come to me, when I tried to write something, of which I had no previous recollection; for I had not then read many books. Our everyday lives are replete with such subtle voices harking back in admonition against, or in praise of, past experiences being similarly repeated.

There are child geniuses who show extraordinary ability at the piano or at composition or at art or at writing or at mechanics, upon the slightest instigation of training, or even spontaneously, without any training. Sir Isaac Newton showed a native proclivity for mechanics. As a boy, he invented a small windmill for grinding wheat and corn, a water clock run by the force of dropping water, and a sundial. He went on to discover such momentous principles as Universal Gravitation, Spectrum Analysis, and the Calculus. Yet, he said of himself just before his death, "I do not know what I may appear to the world, but to myself I seem to have been only like a boy playing on the seashore, and diverting myself in now and then finding a smoother pebble or a prettier shell than ordinary, whilst the great ocean of truth lay all undiscovered before me." I believe that Newton had, indeed, "played on the seashore" in many previous lifetimes and that, compared to what we shall ultimately discover, his principles, albeit momentous, are relatively those of the universe's child.

Another prodigy was Felix Mendelssohn, the great composer. He showed unusual musical talent at an early age, making his first public appearance as a pianist at the age of nine. He also began composing at this early age. Most of us would be surprised to have his gift at any age of life.

Living today is a young Italian, age twelve, who could play any tune he heard on the piano at age 6. At that age he had never had a music lesson. The ability is definitely innate. His name is Enrico Fagnoni, from a family in the village of Aversa, Italy. Enrico Simonetti, conductor of the Italian

Radio and Television Light Orchestra, thought the boy's talent truly frightening in that little Enrico had no musical training yet displayed great musical strength and feeling. Renata Cortiglinone, famous music instructor, hailed Enrico as a genius unequaled during his 25 years of instruction.

Maestro Fagnoni plays equally well in classical, jazz, pop and modern music, drawing from a large repertoire. Enrico's father, Franco Fagnoni, says that his son's talent stems from the memory in that Enrico can play any song heard on the piano…. [For source see bibliography notes below.]

Alfred Lord Tennyson noted that throughout his childhood and adolescence he found himself dramatically issuing proclamations about the grandeur of life, nature and history. These utterances came welling up from his subconscious. He had the poetic inclination and ability from his earliest hours and sought always to channel his expressions through words. Such a dramatic sense as he displayed in his poem "Ulysses" is not to be acquired in one lifetime only, but from the mind's elevation to the perspective which views many past lifetimes, each naturally evolving into its successor and all together giving the feeling of that *One Lifetime*, which is the history of life and of the universe itself. Tennyson's elevation, his enlightenment, came from the history, not of mere decades, but of hundreds of thousands, perhaps millions of years. For his feelings were eternal and not bogged down in the immediate and short stretch of his own lifetime. Tennyson's example, along with Fagnoni's, strongly suggest reincarnation. But there are much more intuitive proofs.

It is inconceivable to me that I should ever cease to exist, just as it is inconceivable that I ever started to exist, or that once I did not exist. Nearly every child, when he begins to ask questions, asks where he came from. He knows intuitively that he must have come from somewhere—and he is absolutely right! He suffers amnesia, perhaps due to the shock of being born, and cannot remember specifically the interim between his last life and his new life—or his last life itself. But he does retain the certain memory that there was a past existence beyond what he presently remembers, beyond even his present birth. If his parents stupidly answer that he came only from his mother's stomach, they are evading the question. They should confess that they are as ignorant of the exact answer as the child himself and that the answer is a holy mystery which should be considered only with the most sober reverence. If I were a parent, I would suggest to the child that God and nature caused him to forget who and where he had been so that he could discover more who he truly is in this life. I would explain that past attachments may have clouded this perfect and universal identity, that of a perfectly realized child of God. But never would I simply deny that this child ever existed before his birth and state with much parental authority that he is definitely a creation of his mother and father. For the parents are the "gateway," not the creators of their offspring….

Perhaps the most direct proof of reincarnation lies in hypnosis. Certain patients who are able to go extraordinarily deep into trance can recall their prebirth "life" both in the interim between lives in the spiritual dimension and in their past life on Earth. For all experience is stored down to every minute detail—as the total experience—within the mind; and, if one overcomes the amnesia which blocks the precise memory of his past lives, he may remember these just as he remembers experiences of his early youth. Many cases other than the Bridey Murphy case, investigated by Morey Bernstein, have been conducted. And this hypnotic recollection of past lives is, now, quite common in the world. Even in my rural area, I know several people who believe they have discovered their past identity or identities through hypnosis.

The reason for our forgetfulness of past identities may be found in the very purpose of birth, which is renovation, a new chance to overcome one's past failures. Hence, it is advantageous to start life with an unattached identity to be newly formed in a better way throughout the course of one's lifetime. However, sometimes, under hypnosis, one can temporarily recall and even reassume a past identity.

Bridey Murphy was able to recall such specifics from her past environment in nineteenth-century Ireland as to prove—after years of archive research by Morey Bernstein—the accuracy of her account. She described roads long nonexistent, shops and the names of their owners, all long forgotten by the world but still indicated on old maps or in archives. Using hypnotic suggestion Mr. Bernstein was able to induce her to dance a genuine Irish jig. Indeed, Mr. Bernstein painstakingly derived strong evidence for reincarnation, and it is, in part, due to the scandalous and biased account of *Life* magazine that people sometimes scoff at the mention of Bridey Murphy.

There are cases on record of children who speak foreign languages without having been taught them, and of children who remember and assume their immediately past identity. In India a child even returned to the family he had most recently departed. Dr. Ian Stevenson also ran across the case of a young boy in India, one Parod, who spoke English words untaught at 2 ½-years of age.

Unyielding belief in reincarnation is found in most of the people of the world: the Indians, both East and West, the Orientals, and most natives who live close to the rhythm of Nature. The Druse of the Near East and the Tlingit Indians of Alaska accept it as a natural occurrence and try to figure out who their babies were. And, of course, the Hindus and Buddhists both believe in it, though in slightly different ways. The Tibetans reinstall their lamas through the aid of vigorous tests for reincarnation. The present exiled Dalai Lama of Tibet is on his thirteenth reincarnation as high lama. He passed a stringent test to verify his reincarnation. In this test he recognized, among other things, the former Dalai Lama's rosary, walking stick, and drum.

Maybe animals intuitively realize reincarnation. This may help to explain their great self-sacrificial, species preservation instinct, and even our own. Indeed, if one views the theory of evolution from a reincarnative standpoint, assuming that species are soul groups reincarnating together, then the outlook on the fossil record and on the behavior of living species changes, for it takes on greater meaning.

Extinct forebears may reappear within a species. Often in hybrid crosses extinct species, or souls, are called to life. Such was the case of the Tarpan, or European Forest Horse. The horse had been extinct since the 1800's until scientists at Hollebrun Zoo in Munich, Germany, "developed a process of back breeding which produced a small horse in the 1950s that looks like the ancient Tarpan." The souls of this species had taken this rare opportunity to manifest themselves. How many souls are there in the spiritual dimension who are not able to enter unless they evolve spiritually so as to compatibly manifest themselves through some existing species?

That extinct souls, or individuals, do manifest themselves within a closely-related, presently existing species is again evinced in nature as Darwin's work suggests:

"Domestic races of the same species differ from each other in the same manner as do the closely allied species of the same genus in a state of nature, but the differences in most cases are less in degree. This must be admitted as true, for the domestic races of many animals and plants have been ranked by some competent judges as the descendants of aboriginally distinct species." (Darwin, *Origin...* page 21)

Chapter 2

Character Versus Personality

Character is the subconscious soul of a life behind the shallow personality, giving it novel expressions and reserve powers on which to draw. Yet, the conscious personality does not understand the depth and meaning of the character on which it is built. One divines the permanent character of his neighbor by trends and signs of the personality, and by the permanent features of the body, particularly the head and face. For the character is the personality of the immortal, ancient life, while this life's personality is but a tiny addition to a vast and immortal one.

Character shows the permanent and lasting traits of the soul established over the millennia. The personality of this life adopts certain expressions of its character while suppressing others. Also, the personality pushes the soul into, heretofore, unknown molds: in this way it expands the mighty character. For life continually tries to overcome itself, that is, its present condition, and to expand into new dimensions of appreciation and ability.

When the soul expands its personality into new molds which expand the mind, then true soul progress is made; but when it "shrinks within itself," adopting past habits which the immortal character wishes to overcome, then the life flounders in the mud of its past. It must suffer the consequences of such a mistake that it might learn the greater lesson. The despair which comes when one realizes that he has betrayed his higher self and has not lived right at the very "tip-top" of his soul-evolution can throw a man into sincere repentance and cause him to shrug off small, nasty, and clinging habits.

To listen to the voice of one's God-attuned soul from the very first time it presents itself is the ideal and fortunate way to progress; but progress is also made by making a mistake, suffering the consequences of the law, and then learning a lesson. And all experience has a lesson. Time measures progress; there is no real, only apparent, regression.

Chapter 3

The Love between Mates as the Medium for Spiritual Incarnation

The unique ethos of love between two particular mates is the gate for the incarnation of one or more certain disincarnate souls. Only those souls who harmonize with this love, who share this love also, can enter via the union of these two mates.

This love is more specific for the higher evolved forms of life. In Man, commonly only one soul is permitted birth at a time. Man's love is highly specific. Only that one soul in the universe who is uniquely suited to the vibration of love of the parents can enter the womb of the mother, through the union of one certain sperm and one certain egg.

Now, "Love is a many-splendored thing." The magnetic attraction between male and female *coupled* with that specific matching of soul mates is magically wonderful, for it involves that which is most basic in life: that fine love which comprises individuality… and its expression in life, its partial fulfillment. For mates inter-express their unique natures, and they relate and exchange soul qualities so as to learn from one another. Yes, love is a teaching and learning process, so much more than people have thought! For in love the essences of character created by all past living are intercommunicated.

And, truly, the joining of male and female is much more than a crass act—though it can be much cheapened through insincerity and debasing lust. It is, above all else, a spiritual process. But, like all things spiritual, it has physical effects, physical expressions. The union of bodies is a symbol of the union, or communication, of souls. When this union takes place, other disincarnate souls are attracted by the certain pitch of love being broadcast and by the opportunity this love provides to incarnate.

Those souls of close relation to the mother and father and in tune with their fine degree and shade of love gather around the mating. This they do in the transcendent dimension of the spiritual ether, which is all about us. At the moment of fertilization, one particular soul is able to enter into the unified egg and sperm. From this point on, the soul psychokinetically directs its physical manifestation through the genetic mechanisms available.

Love is, above all, spiritual; but it manifests itself as a vibration. This vibration varies in frequency and in pattern according to the particular atmosphere between the lovers. It allows the union of only those sperm and eggs which correspond to it. This it does by energizing those sperm in molecular harmony with its vibration. This may occur by a principle similar to the energizing of the laser light beam, as also occurs in rubies.

Any body can be viewed as a vibration of energy. For when physicists and chemists probe into the basic nature of matter, they find it filled with an exuberant motion—indeed, it is like congealed energy straining to free itself. Electrons swarm at a fantastic rate and form different energy levels, or orbits, about the nucleus. This they do as a "probability of presence," not as a planetary type of orbit. Without energy the reactive and evolving physical universe would not be possible. Matter would simply collapse.

Now, the nature of energy itself is a rather intangible one. Like Spirit, it is hard to pin down. It has much the nature of light, or electromagnetic vibration, which is an alteration of magnetic polarities in energy fields, propagated throughout space. Light, of course, is energy too—in, perhaps, its purest form. But we can see only a tiny fraction of the beautiful, spherically radiating energy which lights up the universe. Yet it exists nonetheless

Visible light lies between the infrared and ultraviolet rays. Beyond the ultraviolet lie the X-rays, and cosmic rays, which are of successively higher frequencies. Below the infrared rays, or typical heat rays, lie the radio waves and alternating electric current of extremely slow pulsations. But all these are basically the same phenomenon: electromagnetic vibration, mainly in colors we not only do not know the names of, but have not seen.

Now, I suggest that spirits could manifest through the form of electromagnetic vibrations which are unseen to the normal human eye. These vibrations fill space; and everywhere there are energy fields. Perhaps, spirits, upon death, are transfigured from one place to a faster or slower plane of vibration where their bodies continue as light forms unseen by the living. Indeed, there could exist whole dimensions with manifest beings sensible to the frequencies of their respective dimensions. These worlds could permeate our very world and go unnoticed because we have not the sensual apparatus to perceive them. Perhaps, these energy forms, manifesting in these higher frequencies, influence the molecular activities of the DNA molecules in the chromosomes of the sperm and ova. Indeed, a spirit himself could direct his own manifestation by a harmonization with, and its consequent energization of, those genetic materials capable of manifesting his characteristics and capabilities. Perhaps, the aura, or invisible electromagnetic field about every living creature, is this unseen light form in which the soul passes on to a higher dimension after death. Through the agency of this energy, the souls could again manifest into the material plane.

Chapter 4

Life's Progress with Experience

The soul is displaced in an evolutionary direction with each reincarnative cycle. So we have, as it were, a spiral along which we see, above and beyond the periodic, cyclic changes, an overall cumulative change. We see an increasing complexification of the soul; for the soul becomes more protean, or all-capable, synthesizing its past abilities into a concerted capability. Men are prime examples of this, for their hands, their upright stance, their brain, their stereoscopic vision, etc., allow such versatility—which versatility springs basically from their intricate and diverse past spiritual evolutions. Over many past lives each man has, most likely, been a hunter, a gatherer, a farmer, a warrior, a sailor, a craftsman, an artist, a maker of clothes, houses, and tools, a story-teller, a singer of songs, a musician, a leader of men, a follower, a woman, and much else besides.

With each reincarnation, the soul comes to reflect over a vaster span of experience, from which he learns lessons, draws conclusions, and alters his image of self and, so, his body. It is one's living, one's thinking of thoughts from moment to moment, one's encountering of external objects day to day, which composes the basic transformation of life. This concept is so basic, yet it continues to elude Western man.

Life's progress with experience is cogently expressed in the evolution of the [so-called] primitive forms of life. See how the protozoan evolved into the jellyfish-like organism: and the jellyfish-like organism, into the starfish-like organism; and the starfish-like organism into the fish. See how it was a cumulative progress, i.e., the succeeding being more complex than the preceding, a synthesis and a transcendence of it.…

All of life's changes have their base within the transpiring of the spirit and nowhere else. Reason, purpose, and learning are exemplified in all of life's actions and forms, which are learned responses to the environment in accordance with the desire to live and to manifest more and more totally the capability, expression, and individuality of each and every soul.

The faculty of reason is ever at work, reflecting back over the vast reservoir of one's experience, comparing each and every new experience with all the others in the past to see in what ways it is but a confirmation and repetition of the past or in what manner it is an unprecedented addition to it. With each new moment the psyche is drawing a new overall conclusion on life and universe; and by this his self is altered, imperceptibly from moment to moment, but firmly, permanently, and quite noticeably when observed over a wider span of time. Often great insights come to the soul which change him significantly in the "twinkling of his eyes," but upon analysis this change is often seen to be a response to mounting pressures of environment or to long accumulating trends in his experience. The moment of insight is the moment of logic's action, the moment of decision and of change, when—in an instant—the soul perceives the root of its troubles and makes the change to adopt novel forms. Thus, all true mutations come about.…

Music is the song of yearning for one's total self. Thus, birds sing and animals of many sorts howl for their mates. Music is spun of the substance of dreams, yet it emerges from the vast ocean of soul experience. All sounds that meet one's ear are as music. There is, indeed, magic in the air! If one would only become still and listen, he would hear in random noises the echoes of the mightiest and most profound—as well as the most delicate and subtle—of melodies. Sometimes they come to me, welling up from my inner soul and blending with all beings and things that surround me—giving me great joy to realize that in this magnificent melody is embodied the precise state of my present being in relation to all the world about me. I hear it echoing down throughout the halls of time, yet beckoning, too, into the looming Future. Every once in a great, great while, one enters into the stillness with senses alive. Then one truly hears the meaning of life coming through all the "random" sounds which impinge upon his psyche.

So it is with random colors or forms, and the meaning of art in the natural world: one learns by being still, opening his eyes, and looking. So it is with the deeper, philosophical or religious meanings in life: one learns by making of his senses clear channels for the external to enter and be transformed by, or to itself transform, the inner psyche toward the ideal. One perceives philosophical significances quite often by way of the senses, but the meaning itself is something in addition to these senses: a sixth sense, as it were, but really, all senses in one—yet more. Every once in a while, one becomes still, his mind opens to *all*, and he opens to the great atmosphere of time which surrounds the present and every being or object in it. Then he hears universal harmonies and is called up to join in independently above and beyond that which is *now* in order to fulfill the promise he hears voiced in the melody. Such is a rare and radiant moment in the river of life's experience. It gives one purpose in life and a direction—a role in the panorama of all of life's characters.

Chapter 5

Inspirational Influence on the Evolution of Life

The whole of life listens in the stillness of each universal heartbeat for some precious chord thrown off from the highest heaven, from the very harp of God—which harp is the whole universe. And to whichever strains of this divine melody beings harken, they proceed to dance, and this dance is called living. For without the inspiration to express what one has heard in his inner psyche, there can be no life; for there is no desire to rise up in the morning or even to be born.

Inspiration is the primary cause of life's movement. The environment is but the necessary obstacle through which it must move, and it requires great inspiration in order to desire this movement. For the psyche must glimpse a supernal world, the fulfillment of all his hopes and strivings, at the far end of the labors he must pass through. For life is, in essence, nothing other than a certain fine degree of love hovering whimperingly over its external circumstances and, once in a great while, coming compulsively to the fore to manifest that expression which is truth! So, if the psyche, whether this be of man or beast or plant, cannot glimpse, through the murky waters, the shadows, and the mists, the object of its adoration, then it will have no desire to move, to love, to hunt, to kill, to reproduce, or even to heave that sigh which is the continuance of life itself. Inspiration is the true force of life, for life is spirit.…

When I think of the person of Christ, I envision a vast, extending desert with mountains and hills and wide, flat valleys, all dazzling white and shimmering with heat waves and the sparkles of millions and billions of individual sand crystals. I perceive a noble, tall figure of a man in flowing white robes on the peak of a far-reaching mountain range. His character has grown out of an ancient past, a Hebrew lineage of much mystery. He was vital to many of the momentous times of the past. He is facing the sun and has his arms and radiant countenance uplifted in praise [of God] and in blessing of the entire Earth. As he listens in the desert stillness, he hears the moanings of the sands and the wind, and his mind receives subtle and ancient impressions from civilizations and eras long gone. Yet, these impressions are of universal import, allowing him to peer into the looming future. He is a locus of countless rays of all the colors of the rainbow, which, integrated, form a whiteness that is unearthly, ethereal, *out-dazzling* even the shimmering, desert sands. And these lights of all visible and *invisible* colors radiate in all directions to form a perfect sphere communicating with all parts of the universe. And from his person in relationship to *all*, there arises the most noble and universal music, laden with feeling, import, and intent. In this scene, Christ is speaking to the whole world of people through all channels, those that are plainly perceived through the senses: sight, sound, touch, taste, and smell, and those that can be received through the subconscious alone.…

The universe of beings, all spirits, manifest or unmanifest, is a perpetual state of mind. And the state of mind of each is the product of its interrelationship to that of all others. So all are inextricably bound and cannot find their being save in the Whole of Being. For each is dependent for his condition of life, his thoughts, the substances of his life, upon the universe of the harmonies which are the thoughts thrown out by all beings.

All of the vast ocean of life forms, since the very beginning, has been inspired up out of the darkness by virtue of one omniscient, ever-perfect, light-shedding being, whose name is God. By shedding this psychic light on different parts of the Total Self in different souls and by augmenting or shutting off this light, God has formed the plant and animal kingdoms and each subphylum, class, family, or species in them. All this He has done through the individual; for the individual spirit is the basic unit—not the material chromosomes—of all of life's vast evolution. God divides and separates with His Light, by the directions he lets it shine to, and in the manner He shuts it off to some while letting it augment to others. God governs from the highest order of Reality, by a direct link with the inmost being of everyone.

God is able to do all this because He possesses the Total Self. So, by His direct communicative link to each of us, He gives each to see a unique portion of the Total Self which is the same for all. This unique portion each expresses in his character, his body, etc.

There are groups of souls who have received much the same portions of the Total Self. These are species. Yet, each individual in each species has a slightly different portion than his neighbor; and this portion was given to him in a different manner through different circumstances than the manner and circumstances of his neighbor. For no two of us can be at the same exact spot at the same exact instant. So, by dint of our relative juxtapositions, each sees the universe from a different angle. And, so it is throughout time; each follows a unique path. And there is always only one possible path for each. This path develops a manner or character within the individual which is uniquely his own and which inclines him to continue on his certain path which it is his destiny to follow. Truly, there will come a time at the End of the Universe when all these paths shall converge at the selfsame spot. Then all our journeyings shall be over, and the Eternal Glory shall resume.

Chapter 6

Inspiration through Juxtaposition of the Environment

How often it is through our surroundings that we learn what is the truer! Even in the clouds of the sky are drawn faces of exquisite design. If one would but look for the meaning in all so-called "random" things, such as the clouds of the sky, the sound of rain as it drops on roof and window pane, etc., he would find much of the novel each day. Life would take on a new dimension.

Past times have been a psychological jungle through which I have struggled. Each place, each episode, each epoch of my life is suffused with a unique sense of aliveness, or ethos, which emanates from all the objects, people, animals, plants, mountains, rivers, sounds, smells, and sights I have encountered. And it is not what I did or build or learned or accomplished quantitatively which is of lasting and real value from those past days, but only some fine ethos which emanates from the composite of my experience while from no one thing in particular. The essence of past days often comes to me through poetry, literature, or music, for these trigger an inner harmonization with my past ethos. This harmony may arise from a life lived in another time and culture.

Often, I reflect on how my environment has changed with the episodes of my life. With each new place, my mental outlook has altered. Subtle messages have been imprinted on me by my surroundings.

It seems that while I lived in the forest, my life breathed with the sighing of the trees, and my soul smoldered with the red, somber sunsets which stretched out between two mountains with ruby redness far down to the horizon, into the very Pacific Ocean herself. Only the poet in me can describe what it meant to live then in my childhood. My home and my life, which were my feeling, were in all the trees I daily passed, in the pear and apple orchard, in the valley, in the soft puffs of cloud drifting east, in my grand wooden house and in the oak tree at its side. And let me not forget my loving parents and the dogs and horse who were my constant, loyal companions. All these aspects are pure poetry; they composed a meaning in my life which now I recall with such nostalgia….

[Now, here is a description from my later youth. Location is east of the Sierra Nevada in Carson Valley, Nevada.]

The massive, towering South Carolina poplars around my house are a source of constant refreshment and beauty to me. Some of them tower one hundred-and-twenty-five feet above the lawn. Their thick sprawling limbs, which produce so many large green leaves, seem like fingers of a hand out-reached to the sun asking for light. And, indeed, this is what they are doing. These eight giants, when I sit in their shade or view them from a distance, transport me to a Gargantuan world. When the wind flutters through their myriad leaves, the lambent light sparkles around, and the trees gently, but massively, sway, I think of great symphonies I have heard, poems I have read: of all ecstatic feelings I have had. And I think of life… each soul a leaf… reaching throughout evolution for the Eternal!…

Another remarkable case of meaning conveyed through environment was my revelation of the Spiritual Evolution in a small elm tree in Berkeley, California. The elm actually led me to write this book. One bright and sunny day around noon, as I was walking home from classes, I perceived, in this simple upright tree, a spirit, or soul, that had risen throughout the history of life by repeated incarnations. I perceived so clearly and intuitively the reincarnative, or spiritual, transformation this tree, or myself, or any creature, had gone through in order to be where he is at present, that I was in ecstasy. I peered into the vaster dimension of life, and it gave such a logic and meaning to all that I had been learning in school, and to my life, and to the relationship of all lives about me, that I was "floating on air" in a state of pure ecstasy. My sensitivity to the everyday light of the sun became enhanced so that it dazzled my vision, but was so pure white and crystalline as to be of supreme beauty. By the time I entered my boarding house I was speechless with rapture; all I did was to lie down and muse on this new birth of my soul. For from that moment on, all the world with its creatures was a different place: a place for the free growth of the soul, where each body was imbued with ancient, precious meanings as to how its soul had journeyed throughout all the epochs of Earth's time, transforming itself gradually into its present manifestation. All this I had conveyed to my soul by this simple, young tree. Through it I gained perhaps the most important insight of my life.

I am sure that every experience has a particular meaning. But the significance usually comes to my conscious only upon subsequent reflection. Yes, it is often far in the future that the true beauty and significances of the present come to the mind. Just last night, before I dozed off, I was impressed with how romantic my motorcycle trip along the Dalmatian coast had been: an atmosphere of the whole of Yugoslavia permeated my soul. The whiteness of the looming Adriatic cliffs flashed through my spirit, as did the panorama I had seen at sunset looking out over the Adriatic Sea to those long, shark-like islands that skirt the coast. The rough, unshaven, earnest faces of the peasants and their sparsely-covered, dry, brown fields came to me. My feasts on wild pomegranate and dry figs (on which I had practically subsisted) flashed by me also. The heartfelt songs these people would sing I could almost hear again. I thought, too, of the young Britisher who had traveled along with me in southern Yugoslavia… of his pert and curious manner and the lilt of his voice. The etheric island-town of *Sve Stephan* and the snowy Southern Alps and their hospitable peasants also came to me. Many other experiences of this part of my journey flashed instantaneously across my mind. All these seemed to blend into an overall impression like a particular song or symphony, novel or play. At this moment of dreaming and reflection, in India, a land far-distant and far-different from Yugoslavia, I reaped the true meaning and pleasure I had sought two months earlier in Yugoslavia. This supreme moment was worth all the sickness, weariness, and effort put forth in traveling through that country. And even this latter, the hardship lent an essential ingredient to the ethos.

Yes, at these moments of high reflection, I can affirm that there is a poetry in the "random" sequence of life's events. But it comes like a shock wave to my conscious long after the jet of NOW has zoomed past. These past experiences well up out of my subconscious, where they exist forever. They group together to form epochs of my life, and they appear in my conscious as intellectual "fragrances." There is not a thing I have ever seen, heard, smelled, tasted, felt, or experienced in any way, [that] is not part of some mental fragrance. For, when I look into my past, I see that it is all a *state of mind*, which changes simultaneously with its external environment as it grows. There is nothing random, nothing absurd, when I enter into these states of high reflectivity. And even though all of my experience does not then coalesce into a single pearl of omniscience, yet I realize that this is only due to my transient understanding. When the mists of time have cleared, then I shall see the whole of my universal life throughout the epochs and millennial of time—I shall see it all as One!…

For even though effective change may seem the hardest think in the world to bring about, it is surely the most *inevitable!* Perhaps this is why it is resisted so stubbornly. For it is the glorious Future which draws us forth by the magnetism of its beautiful potentials and the allure of its Perfect ideal. We are not always driven by the machines of past habits, no matter how long they have continued. The longer some narrow and blind way has been, the more certain and soon shall be its change!

But this is not to say that all permanent things must fall. It is, rather, the long-standing ways of ignorance, insensitivity, and lack of conscience which must fall. Such ways are presently being exhibited by mankind to his fellow creature. And man's relationship to Nature is now more disgusting than ever! His perverted sense of "civilization" or "progress" is the long-standing way which must fall. For it means the artificialization of the world. But the relatively permanent natural phenomena, such as the sun, the moon, and the stars; and the cycles of their motions—they all shine on and will until someday their full significance is understood. (And it is now *only the Beginning!*)

For the Truth is like the sun: it shines every day in its fullest brilliance. But who, yet, has been born that can open his eyes to receive its full radiance without being absolutely dazzled?!…

One may argue that it is man's scientific method which is responsible for his understanding of the world. But I still ask the question: what evolutionary process led him to value the scientific method, or logical thought itself? Certainly, in developing this logic, it was his teacher Nature whom he was emulating. For it is the logic and order inherent in the world which Man reflects in the workings of his mind. By copying his teacher, he has discovered his greater self, thus proving again that the world is the medium of spiritual evolution. And who is the teacher who works through all the mediums of the world but that Supreme and never-fallen Spirit: God?

Chapter 7

The Mind is a Dimension unto Itself

In this vast world with its oceans and mountain peaks, its myriad fish and creatures of the air, its viruses and its men, and in all their history throughout time, all phenomena are inextricably bound to and one with their corresponding ideas within the Total Mind, or Spirit. For Spirit is a dimension, just as is space or time. And just as time includes space, so does the spirit include all time, and, so, all space. The spirit is the one all-permeating, single unity of all things and processes and dimensions.

All objects in space—all space itself—travel in time and are reflections in their conditions and juxtapositions of the momentary universal state of mind. And since all time is within the spirit, so is all space, for time is made up of changing spatial events [yet contains a transcendent quality unique to time itself]. Spirit is the subtle essence of all things: it is the existence (by definition) of the universe. It is of a radically different nature from space-time, for it is pure sensitivity, not only to things of space-time, but also to things purely of the spirit. This latter, self-sensitivity, gives rise to will-power.

Perhaps, someday, one of the chief defining characteristics of spirit shall be recognized as "the ability to indwell any substance or energy." In other works, it will be seen that the spirit can "hop a light beam" and travel to the remotest galaxy, or impregnate the densest core of any planet or any star with life and awareness. But in addition to this, it will be seen that the spirit can transcend all physical reality and skip from one end of the universe to the other much faster than the speed of light—as quickly as thought! Perhaps it will do this by an inner realization of what always was, in fact, within itself.

All physical things: atoms, molecules, volcanoes, galaxies, etc., are understandable to the spirit. There exists, as it were, a duplicate universe: one of things physical, the other of physical things understood and made spiritual. I say that these are not two separate and duplicate universes but one, and that the reason all physical things and processes can be understood is that they have their essence within the dimension of the spirit. Spirit is a dimension inclusive, yet transcendent, of all the physical. Within the Total Mind, the potential of each of us, all of the universe and its evolution are contained, for the substance of spirit permeates and unites It All. Just as the Hindus would say:

that all is within the Brahma, the Perfectly and, so, Completely Enlightened Spirit: that which God forever embodies and retains (so that we might be inspired through Him).

When the poet describes the sea and its vastness, the air and its overwhelming sway over all the land, the vastness of space, and the eternity of time, his spirit partakes something of the essence of these: it reaches out into the vast expanses, and back into the dim eons of the past or stretches into the looming future. It realizes intuitively its tie with all that lies within reality. This awakening to one's unity with the universe is the joy, power, and prestige of the poet: this feeling of unity with universe, this reflection of one's state of mind in the things of nature, this euphoric, dreamlike state is an exalting ecstasy such as poetry can produce. Here is an example of such a feeling.

Once on a grey and cloudy day in the San Francisco Bay region I lay down upon a table to watch a legion of clouds which passed upon their way from ocean to mountain. And, as I peered upon a billowy cloud proceeding majestically inland, it seemed I not only saw it but that I perceived it within myself, that my spirit extended out to enclose it and that I became the cloud and proceeded majestically with it. Far more than seeing was this experience; rather it was like a clairvoyance, like an illumination of my conscious unto its greater self, unto that part which reached out to include the cloud rolling above me. I became its very existence. That vacuum within myself filled....

Music is a great key by which to unlock the inwardness of the universe. It is inherent in the omnipresent rhythm of nature: in the motions of the waves, the clouds, the wind, the motions of the subatomic particles, such as the perfect elasticity of the electron, the revolutions and rotations of the moon, planets, sun, and stars, etc. According to nature's rhythm, life evolves, changing somewhat with each successive cycle, in a universal direction, which is toward greater sensitivity and the perfect, all-capable, omniscient state of mind. Life evolves according to a natural rhythmic unfolding from lesser aliveness of the components of its spirit to greater activation of these. There is a universal rhythm to which a life may be uplifted, and to It, all beings, as well as all things, sway!

Certainly in music there is reflected *living* in all its vicissitudes, in all its doldrums, in all its triumphant moments, in all its agonies and its ecstasies… rendering them all—the composite—so undeniably beautiful. This is one of the ways in which spiritual evolution is compactly expressed. Other ways are those of the painter, the artist, the sculptor, the conceptualizer, and the story-teller. But for me at present, music seems best to connote life in all its brightest moments or its darkest hours and in all the hues, shades, and degrees in between! It seems to unite me with all lives of all times!…

I feel a sweeping transformation within my spirit in this day and age and observe it in my fellow man. It is like a dilation of the mind, an enhancement of perspective by which I view the whole of reality. There is a greater freedom come upon the minds of the Fallen. This is seen in the unconventionality of this generation; but, too often, it is used as an excuse to degrade the self, so that the self becomes dark and a slave of sin. But, ideally, this looseness should be used to obtain the real freedom which is: to be [consciously realize] more one's higher and truer self, one's total self. For sin is a betrayal of one's higher and total self, a parasite of virtue; it must always lead to frustration, misery, and disharmony in one's life. The one who shall, truly, profit from this newly given freedom is the one who shall retain and use all the virtues of the past forged into a concerted instrument by which to obtain a Greater Single Virtue which shall be the culmination and the transcendence of all those previously acquired. This virtue shall, indeed, be an enhanced quality of what the person is inside, and it shall be manifested in all his works, in all his expressions, from those of his own body to those of the creations of his hands. All these shall emanate his appreciation of the universe, for they shall be lighted by the love of his understanding of such and his faith in its perfection when viewed all-inclusively.

In order to stand up, one must hold his head in the air and fight the gravity which pulls him down. But without the gravity, he could not stand up at all, for he would have no standard by which to orient himself. No, he would be without form. So it is with evil and the temptations to lower our standards in life: they give us something to fight against, and they crush in us all inferior traits, so that only the purest and strongest prevail. They make it a challenge for life to aspire to its very highest ideals in the sky… the misty sky whose angels are glimpsed from time to time through the murk of our befogged minds. So we must push on into new and untried modes of life, every striving after the very highest of our ideals for the self and for the world.…

For truly, the spirit is a dimension unto itself; it cannot possibly be defined in terms of any physical dimension alone. It is transcendent of space-time and matter, though it expresses itself through the modes of both. Yet, all things physical can be assumed into spiritual cognizance.

Surely Spirit is the independent essence of all these lesser dimensions. Surely it is a dimension unto itself and is truly the only dimension: all-inclusive, unified, and radiant, forever and ever! Realization of this brings liberation from incompleteness of self and resumption of eternal bliss. Toward this self-same realization does all of life, from minute diatom to majestic saint, proceed.

And as life becomes more honest, so it approaches the Glory!

Chapter 8

The Conservation of Existence

Spiritual Existence is conserved in the universe just as are matter and energy. Though the soul may change form, yet its abiding essence, what you are and I am, remains forever. The many forms are what we see as all the lives incarnate upon Earth. Yet, there were forms here a hundred, a thousand, a million, or a billion years ago; and, though these forms were noticeably different between one time and another, yet they were ever sparked into action and being by the spiritual "will to express" of each soul. And it is these wills, these spirits, who abide forever, for they all find their source of continuance in the *selfsame* Center of Universal Being, toward which they all proceed.

Every day where I live, many births evince the entrance of spiritual beings into my realm, the Earth. But I see other bodies give up the spark of life and lose all form and function. I see these bodies return to dust. Truly, these no longer even deserve to be called bodies: for where is the form and expression of the spirit? It has departed to that same higher, unknown realm from which came the newborn babe. Yes, many are entering in; many: departing. From whence come they; to whence do they return? All the lives and deaths born and died are evidence of a greater dimension to which we here below have lost the awareness.

Yet, this greater dimension is ever with us; we "live, breathe, and have our being" in it, for it is substance of mind, spiritual ether. To it we owe existence itself, for we compose it. Is this so hard to fathom? Why, it is the most apparent of all things… and, maybe, for just this reason, [for some stubborn souls] the hardest to realize.

The reason departed beings are no longer visible to us is that we have blotted out of our spirits the awareness of the vaster realm in which they abide—the Great Beyond. We have subjugated our minds to include only what we call the "physical universe," the universe of our sensation. And, perhaps, *there is* an electromagnetic manifestation of departed spirits in an unseen dimension. Yet, there is so much more to reality than just the physical. There are things purely spiritual: things envisioned by poets, musicians, artists, priests, visionaries: in short, by dreamers of all sorts.…

I find a proof of immortality of the soul right in my inmost being. For when I (my conscious) am still and listen to that Voice of Truth which proceeds from within (the subconscious) I hear this: "I am immortal, one with all Time. When Time began: that is when I had my birth, if you insist that

I should have a birth! But, really, I am beyond Time and its sickly motion. I am the all-pervading NOW: essence of your life throughout all that which you call Time. I am the Eternal Instant. When your Time ends, then I shall again reign in your mind, for I was and still am and ever will be what you call myself. Yet, I am more than momentary existence, but all moments fused together into one Instant, which is the whole of your spiritual evolution. This Instant shall be the equivalent of the one Idea: the Glory 'out of space, out of time.'…

The reader may again protest: "But how could an ant or a fly… or, or… an *Ameba* (said with distain) have an immortal soul; like *Man* (said with much arrogance)?" To this maddening question (but I will "keep my cool") I would reply: "Please, sir, if you would but take note of a life for once in your life and not just the life of another man? For the other creatures about you are also worth taking note of. Their hearts beat just as do ours. Please observe this ant, for example. It scurries so 'zig-zaggedly' along the ground at our feet. Does not it evince that same fundamental Will which I do, just by speaking to you? The wind pushes it not, nor does it roll like a rock having been pushed by my foot. No, the ant is not pushed or pulled in any way, yet it proceeds of its own accord in defiance of all the known 'mechanistic' laws of Nature. How, indeed, could this ant walk that 'zig-zag' path if it had not an individual will with an individual purpose, just as you or I have? And to have these it must be a mind. Therefore, the ant is surely a mind; the same basic substance as you and I, dear friend… even though it is inspired by [seemingly] different goals and lights than you and I. As for myself, sir, I have no more reason to doubt the existence of this ant's mind, or soul, or spirit, than I have to doubt yours, or my mother's, or my father's, or my sister's, or my brother's. All external personages or creatures from man to ameba give evidence, in their observed behavior, of that self-same quality of mind which I most cherish in myself as the essence of my being. I have no other choice but to assume that these other myriad beings share with me in possessing, or, rather, in *being*, this universal quality of mind.…

For this reason, whenever anyone starts talking to me about God: who He is and what he knows of Him and His universe, I always look him "squarely in the eye" and size him up. For that portion of God, of which one knows, that he "is", that he expresses in his every word, action, or bodily feature—that is his god. But only when he bows his head in humility to the Complete God of the Universe (and we all intuitively know who He is), shall he testify to the True and Living God. For, then, he will speak with love and with the desire to understand what I (who speak with him) have discovered of God, so that he himself might learn of the True and Living God to a greater degree. I, likewise, should listen to my neighbor's unique knowledge of portions of God; and, in mutual love, we should accept what we both have to offer. Yet, we should not hold up our incomplete knowledge as the Truth; rather, together, we should delve into the known and unknown universe with greater and greater degrees of honesty. Then, indeed, shall we have the true love of God in our hearts. For this love will cry out to the Highest for greater blessing and seek to augment itself to the greatest of all loves. It will seek the True and Total God! For true love is a giving and a receiving with gladness: one man to one woman, one father to one son, one mother to one daughter, and (vice-versa), Mankind to all species of Life, all Life to God, and God to All Life. For true love is the abandonment of small self to what is outside of and greater than one's present smallness and incompleteness [of realization]. It is the "reaching-out," the motion, and that discovery which is the very "spark" of life, the reason for living!

Sangay Volcano in eruption Dec. 1989 – All photos © Craig C. Downer

Chapter 9

The One Idea

What in the world, or in dreamland, shall this One idea be like? It shall be like Everything you have ever experienced whether in this world or in dreamland or in "death" lives or in past lives or in the dimmest beginnings of your spiritual evolution. Also, it shall be like all things you are going to experience in the Future. It shall be the One Thing which all these "things" were trying to express but did not succeed in doing… save when joined all together.

If this is still too abstract for you, then I will say of the One Idea that it shall unite all sensations as one. This should not be so hard to conceive, for we do it all the time. Take a particular feeling of beauty, for example. The self-same feeling we may derive either from music, or poetry, or a pleasing fragrance, or an artist's painting, or many, many other things. Thus, we experience the transcendent expression of all music, poetry, art, etc., in the subtlety of our feelings; and it matters not to our minds, at this high plane, through what medium the feeling is derived. Thus, when we feel that Feeling of feelings, then we shall have arrived at the Pure and Essential Beauty of All Things, which Beauty we shall truly BE!

Chapter 10

The Fall and the Rise

From the Oneness, the periphery of Existence fell in all its multitudes. This Fall was like a terrific explosion by which the Center of Being was dispersed into all the components of Total Being. These were separated and dispersed throughout the universe. The physical universe and the space-time continuum served to divide all the various entities and groups thereof. All the energies of the universe were manifested in this radiation from the Center, which corresponded with the birth of all separate beings: they were radiated throughout all the universe, for their conscious minds shrank to occupy only certain sections thereof. And, according to the Nature of this happening, all physical things in the universe reflected the Universal State of Mind contributed to by all beings. Yes, the physical universe was the spiritual ethos' natural reflection and manifestation right from the Beginning.…

Perception of other beings is a way by which the soul can make rapid progress, for he compares his being to theirs and learns what soul-experience they have which he lacks. Through mutual love there is a transference of soul-experience and mutual augmentation, resulting in greater wisdom and perfection of form in the participants. This is the magic of the love between father and mother, and, also, of the love between and among all souls, no matter how diverse. From lifetime to lifetime, one marches from one mate to another, one region to another, etc., until he acquires a vast storehouse of soul capacities, all integrated and expressed anew in his present state of being with each succeeding moment. Yet, each succeeding moment builds on trends set in motion far in the past… since the very beginning.

Yes, evolution is inherent in our moment-to-moment existence: for, as we march on in inner time from idea to idea, we integrate all that is past into the present, which is subsequently integrated into the future. Yes, each succeeding moment is the culmination of all preceding moments: the concerted construction of them all. Many modern psychologists suggest, upon observation, that the mind compares each succeeding idea with all ideas it has experienced in the past, integrating them all so as to give as concerted an expression as possible. But, perfect and wholly integrated expression of being is not to be attained until the end (the One idea). The whole universe, the whole spirit world, the whole of life on Earth (or elsewhere) surges forth in unity toward completion and fulfillment, toward the manifestation of the One Idea [the conscious realization of this] in all minds and in the [externalized expression of the] Entire Physical Universe!

There is only one common Nature by which the whole universe proceeds. This is partially expressed by the laws of gravity, magnetism, electricity, mechanics, relativity, etc., *and* by the laws of the psyche: transcendent expressions of their corresponding physical laws and further expressions in and of the psyche alone. Such laws are of intellectual logic and emotional impulse. Yet, logic and emotion are not divorced from one another, but they are united: what we experience as emotional impulse is really the logic of our greater being, the subconscious [better stated as "superconscious"], as it directs our lesser conscious being toward Completeness. For the mind realizes that all partial ideas are illusions proceeding from the one and only idea: are incomplete expressions of this one. So it moves toward greater synthesis. This is the cause of life as we know it; for, in reality, all living is but the synthesizing of the One Idea. When this synthesis is completed, time will stop and that perfect Stillness shall reign throughout and in all what was once the universe of Space-Time-Mind as we knew it. All is one, A Glorious Sun!

This following poem was written in my early days at Berkeley, California, in the Spring of 1967:

The Sun

In the midst of smothering darkness,
In all its holy starkness,
There burns a holy light
Kept every by His might.
—Yet, though it be night,
'T is dawn to me,
Holding no fright,
But ecstasy.
There is a faint light,
All permeating as Divine Love
Which sublimes to a height,
This world to the far home of the Dove.
In this dawn I want to awaken,
My eternal desire, constantly.
I want to be taken,
There, to home, to be free,
Where everyone is one,
A Glorious Sun!

This poem reflects in feeling what I have attempted to show intellectually. It expresses that yearning for the eternal which is in each individual.

Individuals are different paths, or workings of the universal laws of being. Each soul traverses a different portion of the universe. At each moment he sees a different perspective. He traverses all the parts of the universe in a sequence different from all other souls. His momentary state of being is always uniquely different from that of any of his neighbor's, even his closest of kin; for the combined synthesis of his past soul experiences is always inclusive of additional parts and lacking in other parts when compared with that of his neighbor. And no two people ever experience the same thing in exactly the same way. Only at the End of Time shall all beings converge and [again realizedly] be One, for then they will have each traversed the whole universal circuit, thereby experiencing all aspects thereof. Then, in the mind of each, the synthesis shall be complete and whole. Time shall then stop, for it was but incompleteness waxing toward Completeness. It will have accomplished its purpose.

Chapter 11

God, Fashioner of the Universe

How can life know what it never knew before [since the Fall] unless this knowledge is communicated to it by an all-bright, pure, and omniscient spirit? This one is God, the ever-supreme being of the universe. He it is who, by His shedding of Light, variously as to all the various beings, has inspired the spiritual evolution of the vast kingdom of life on Earth and that of all beings, wherever else in the universe and in the all-pervading spiritual heaven they might dwell.…

The soul's body is transformed as it travels along through time. By the impression of each different place and of each different inhabitant one meets, one's identity is altered. It is as though one were driving in a car through the world, and as he visits different places, his body alters so as to be able to live in these places. And he changes as he moves on, yet retains the capacities he has gained in the places passed by. For a minute, this seems like a nightmare until we realize its purpose and its end. This car journey is equivalent to life, or evolution itself; and its direction is toward the Most Beautiful: Paradise. . .

We, the Fallen, also act according to our natures, as lesser parts of the Complete Nature, by which God ever acts. We cannot go against the nature, so we ever act in harmonization with its laws. However, we can make transit from a lesser order to a greater order of these laws. Never can we escape the Nature, not even God can, yet He includes it all. In a sense, He might rise above it, but not to its negation. In encompassing all of the Nature, God transcends it and, so, is not subject to the confinement we, the Fallen, know. The Divine nature is responsible for all happenings, whether they be at a lower level of molecular energy or at higher levels of human or angelic thought. [Yet, in fact, these are all interrelated and one.]

Yet, it is not as though God were pulling the puppet strings of our thoughts and actions. Rather, the inter-harmonization between God and life is due to the fact that both act according to the Divine Nature of the universe. God is the distributor of lights from off the Most Perfect; we are those who receive His lights and are energized by them. Now, how could God shed His light if He were to lose it: if there were not the Fallen to absorb it and, then, to yield it up to Him again in love? Truly, both God and life are necessary so that the universe might proceed and the Divine Nature therein express itself to the end that the Complete and Exact Expression of such might be manifest throughout the whole of the physical-spiritual universe.

Both God and each spirit contain within their inner being the essence of the Divine Nature. So, it is by expressing ourselves most deeply, most honestly, most completely, and in the maximum possible freedom and fearlessness that we honor the Divine Nature to the highest degree. We honor God who forever preserves this Complete Divine nature in his conscious state of being so that we, the Fallen might again attain our Complete Selves through communion with Him. Yet, both God and the Fallen (the Periphery of Existence) are imperative to the workings of the universe and the Divine Nature (or Holy Spirit) therein.

God must exist in order to preserve Perfection and in order to lead, or to direct, the universe. Within Himself, ever in His highest heaven He keeps consciously alive Omniscience, Omnipotence, and Omnipresence. Because a real individual spirit is in this highest State, communication of salvation is possible to those who fell to near complete annihilation. So, in many varying sequences and with diversely colored lights, God fashions the evolution of the universe of elements and of minds, living and "dead." Also, He fashions the bodies of spirits as reflections of their minds. By giving spirits to perceive and, so, to manifest what they perceive of His Complete Self, He directs evolution. Yet, even He is a part of this evolution, for His actions evolve from those which fashion a lower order of the universe to those which fashion a higher order. He is like a painter who first sketches in the rough outlines, then later adds the fine finishing touches.…

Every soul acknowledges God in his honest, inward self. When the hazards of the world bear heavily down, when one is sick, frustrated, wounded of body and of hope, then it is to the Higher Power, to this Spirit who listens to all the heart's outpourings: to God that the soul prays. When one has been humiliated and admits his shortcomings in dealing with the problems imposed by the world, then God gives Light into the inner capacity of the soul. The soul takes on a new hope, a new patience, and a new manner of doing things. One takes on a new goal for his life—or maybe [rather] the same pure and distant one, but he has new abilities by which to obtain it. This comfort, reassurance, and new incentive is the direct evidence of God's inspiration at work. Those who do not cry out for God's light, but fall back on their own small pride, sink into darkness and are given up to despair and smallness.…

Every soul knows, when he is honest, that God is the Light of his path, or life. He knows that he proceeds toward the Greater Light, far, far into the future, and toward the Divine Image expressed in all mediums. For how could he have changed from a primitive form to his present form unless there were a revealing power at work in his life? Yet, without an inner yearning, a sense of personal destiny, the soul would not have chosen the path it did, absorbing its particularly colored lights along this path.

Yes, the individual, too, is important. He, too, moves the universe; and all the universe of beings hinge upon his actions and depend on him to act. He shares with God in the dance of destruction and creation (transformation) which is life. He is co-creator with God. He creates "living," or history… which is something precious to relive.…

Truly, every living or nonliving soul of Earth or Heaven, is [subject to] a fashioning of [by] God. Yet, there would be no fashioning if the soul did not allow himself to be fashioned along a particular sequence of forms and in a unique manner. This *will* is the individuality and integrity of each and every soul. It is his share in the creation of the universe, his claim to the Glory, and his integrity. This it is which caused the need for spiritual evolution in the first place: the existence of individuals. But in order to have a spiritual evolution, there must have been an original fall or forgetting.…

The *spark* is that glint of pure spirit beyond all the world, yet, without which the world could not proceed. This spark God gives life to see in as many different ways as there are beings. Yet, the essence of the spark is the same for all.

The spark is the "Agony and the Ecstasy," for it is only upon that moment of deepest despair that we are set free, that we are lighted by the transcendent spark of pure spirit and able to share in that magnificent discovery which is the reason for our Fall and all of life's evolution. For it is then that we abandon our smallness and ignorance. It is only when we END, utterly and irretrievably—for all the world can explain—and then, miraculously, begin again, that we know life's essence. Then we behold that which we have never imagined to exist in our old world.

Life is spontaneity and freshness; and Discovery is the reason for living.

Chapter 12

The Divine Nature

There is a Nature by which all phenomena in the spiritual and physical universe proceed. This Nature we observe in the laws of physics, chemistry, biology, evolution, and all the processes of life and of our world. But these latter are but the effects of the greater spiritual laws which govern our mind, emotions, and instincts.

Thinkers of all sorts, throughout the ages, have tried to unlock the logic of their world and to make a mental model of it. This endeavor to understand the world is one and the same with trying to see its soul: the mind which permeates its entirety, from within and from without. By exploring and observing the chemical, biological, or astronomical worlds, men are unlocking hidden recesses of their own minds in order to understand what they observe.

But, just as often, men have discovered great truths, *a priori*, by thinking. Only later have they confirmed their conceptions by observations of the external world. Albert Einstein discovered the theory of relativity by first working largely with the hidden recesses of his own capacity for mathematical logic. He was, in fact, exploring the universe of the mind; and this universe is one of all possible ideas. Subsequently, upon telescopic observations of the Doppler effect of light from a receding star, his astounding theory was corroborated. Space and time seemed to be relative to the speed of light. The mathematical logic of his mind—the potential of any mind—was reflected perfectly in the physical universe....

But, in the last couple centuries, particularly the last, mankind has shamefully neglected the spiritual laws of his own and *all life's* inner being. By his exploitation of Nature and its life communities and his selfish "using" of all forms of life for his physical comfort and surfeit, he has transgressed the great moral laws of the spiritual universe. And these are the first laws, of which the physical laws are but the effects. For spirit is, by the most logical nature, the director of the physical, just as a creature's mind is controller of its body. When man denies compassion and freedom to his spiritual brothers [and sisters], however [so-called] lowly evolved, then he transgresses the laws of love. But no one can long transgress these laws without himself reaping the ill effects. For laws hold and they will reassert themselves! There is a law of universal justice, I feel sure; its effects and statutes resound through my whole being.

One of the main laws is that of the Spiritual over the Physical, or "Mind over Matter." Each and every life is a living testimony to this principle. And, as evolution proceeds, the Spirit asserts itself increasingly over the lower forms of matter, lifting them to higher and higher degrees of expressivity. . . .

In our world at present, we must proceed along those trends already set in motion. These trends must all be resolved to their natural conclusions. As life culminates lower trends, its motion shall be assumed into higher, more all-inclusive laws of vaster motion. For there are lesser laws and greater laws which include the lesser laws. The One Sole Existing Law, or trend, of Universal Evolution transcends all lesser trends. All lesser laws are but incomplete expressions of the One Law. Life on Earth amply illustrates this....

America could take a lesson from these; for technology has enthroned its citizens, but many are using their wealth and comfort for debauch and not for the betterment of the world. For they fail to see the noble purpose of life that transcends all worldly wealth and pleasure, yet, gives a greater satisfaction all of its own. And it is when the soul feels lost and without a higher purpose in life that it submits to the lower, deadening tendencies of evil and of sin: carnal lust, drunkenness, drug abuse, gluttony, lust for power, wealth for its own sake, vainglory, [materialism of all sorts] etc.

Life is change; and change must have some direction, some final or ultimate goal, or else there would be no [reason for] motion at all. If there were no trends, no motions to be completed, no forces to be resolved, and no laws of the spiritual-physical universe, then there would be no guide to living, thinking, and acting: there would be no ultimate nature by and toward which all the universe proceeds toward this Stillness, this complete self-independence. All lesser laws resolve themselves and become components of greater and greater laws, until the One and Only and Greatest Law only prevails over the entire universe. This Law is that the universe must become perfectly and totally resolved and still in Perfection, in Total self-realization. Then Time will stop and only the Holy Spirit will reign in Timeless Eternity.

Have not the myriad basic building blocks of matter followed the law (or trend) of becoming the atom (mainly hydrogen)? And have not the atoms of all the elements united to form molecules? And out of cosmic gases, stars have coalesced. And out of many stars emerged galaxies. Surely, the galaxies themselves follow some prodigious law of Becoming: or resolving into a greater and more all-inclusive unit. Out of the very matter of the Earth, life has arisen. Following successively greater and greater laws to become the single cell, the multicellular organism, the chordate, the land creature, and man. Surely there is abundant evidence of a greater and greater *becoming* seen throughout life— and life's essence, the soul [which ever includes the beings in all diverse forms and species, places and realms—ever united upon Holy Life's Highest Plane]!...

My imagination is full of inexplicable memories from my existence before this life. I have seen myself in my mind's eye in burning desert sands, among a group who dwelt in earthen huts which went underground. I have had a vision which took me to London as a bird, only faster. This was at sunset over the city; and I instinctively clued in on an old Victorian mansion. In this mansion I most clearly and strongly felt the genius of some old man who, like a Darwin, was full of knowledge and wisdom. This impression reached a climax, after which, I was transposed to Egypt, where I saw the Great Sphinx of Gizeh, at the sun's zenith, and perceived, again so clearly and strongly, a very definite meaning [and presence]. Indeed, I know my identity had been partially attached to these edifices, for so much soul-experience came welling up [in] me. I must have lived in both England and Egypt in past lives [and in the land of those burning desert sands]. How far past the Egyptian one was, I don't know–but it was ancient, thousands of years ago. Perhaps I helped to build the Sphinx.

. . . . The joy to change toward the Highest is the Love of the Holy Spirit! And it matters not from what [seemingly] low level the soul aspires.

"References and Notes" at end of The Spiritual Evolution: A Book on Reincarnation and Evolution

Chapter 1, Footnote 4. Charles Darwin, The Origin of Species by Means of Natural Selection: or The Preservation of Favored Races in the Struggle for Life; and The Decent of Man and Selection in Relation to Sex (1859, 1871; reprint, New York: The Modern Library, N.D.), p. 447.

Chapter 1, Footnote 7. Granville Toogood, "Boy Hailed as a Modern Day Mozart," *National Enquirer*, Lantana, Florida: Aug. 18, 1974; p. 4.

Chapter 1, Footnote 9. A. D. Hasler & J. A. Larsen, "The Homing Salmon," *Scientific American* (Aug. 1955).

Chapter 1, Footnote 10. Morey Bernstein, *The Search for Bridey Murphy* (New York: Doubleday, 1956).

Chapter 1, Footnote 12. Ian Stevenson, *Twenty Cases Suggestive of Reincarnation* (New York: American Society for Psychical Research, A.S.P.R 1966).

Chapter 1, Footnote 13. Ian Stevenson, "A Case of Responsive Xenoglossy" (New York: A.S.P.R.).

Chapter 1, Footnote 14. Ian Stevenson, *Twenty Cases Suggestive of Reincarnation*. Parmod of Indian at 2 ½ years spoke English words, untaught. op. cit.

Chapter 1, Footnote 15. P. K. Hitti, "The Origins of the Druse People and Religion with Extracts from Their Sacred Writings," *Columbia University Press*, 1928); I. E. P. Veniaminov, *Reports About the Islands of the Unalaska Districts* (St. Petersburg, Russia: Imperial Academy of Sciences, 1840); Ian Stevenson, "Cultural Patterns in Cases Suggestive of Reincarnation among the Tlingit Indians of Southeastern Alaska," (*Journal A.S.P.R., vol. 60, July 1960).*

Chapter 1, Footnote 17. "Tarpan," *The World Book Encyclopedia* (Chicago: Field Enterprises Educational Corp., 1964).

Chapter 4, Footnote 2. *L'uomo universal* is a term coined by Italian Renaissance humanists, meaning "the universal man," i.e., one with a wide diversity of talents and interests, such as Da Vinci, Michelangelo, [pantheist and free thinker Giordano Bruno] and others.

Chapter 6, Footnote 2. I wrote this part and about two-thirds of this book in the religious settlement of Vrindaban, U.P., India, the birth place of Lord Krishna, considered holy to the Hindus. It is on a plain extending from horizon to horizon and near a smooth, flowing river, the river "Jum'na." Yugoslavia, on the other hand, is more mountainous and rocky, particularly in Dalmatia, along the cliff-bound Adriatic shore, which I skirted on my [large Heinkel touring] motor scooter during the fall of 1970 *en route* to the East [and where I also conceived many concepts that went into my book].

Chapter 9, Footnote 2. *Ohm* is believed by certain Hindus to be the perfect, all-inclusive, all expressive vibration, or sound. It is supposed to be a perfect humming noise. Whole volumes have been written upon *Ohm*, for it is from this universal and all-inclusive vibration that all phenomena are believed to have proceeded.

Chapter 9. Footnote 4. Here, the word *Assumption* is used in the sense of the "assumption of the Virgin Mary," meaning the apotheosis of such. All plurality and diversity of things, qualities, etc., will take on supreme and maximally joyous meaning when they come together in harmony, and are seen only in the greatest of lights.

Chapter 9, Footnote 7. "Love is patient and kind; love is not jealous or boastful; it is no arrogant or rude. Love does not insist on its own way; it is not irritable or resentful; it does not rejoice at wrong, but rejoices in the right. Love bears all things, believes all things, hopes all things, endures all things" (I Corinthians 13:7, Revised Standard Version).

Chapter 9, Footnote 9. Compare George Hegel's (1770—1831) philosophy of the dialectic which states that the thesis and antithesis (in thought) are resolved in the prevailing synthesis. See his *Logic* (1817).

Chapter 10, Footnote 3. It is fairly common knowledge that the mind stores all soul-experience within itself. This allows the hypnotic reliving of such. This storage is manifest materially in the cortex of the brain. Upon electric stimulation of brain cells, the individual experiences past memories in their totality [or so they say]. [Some] Psychologists also verify that the mind compares and integrates each new experience with all those of the past.

Chapter 11, Footnote 2. "But he answered [the tempter Satan], 'it is written, (Deut. 8:3), Man shall not live by bread alone, but by every word that proceeds from the mouth of God.'"—Matthew 4:4, Revised Standard Version.

Chapter 12, Footnote 2. For an intelligent and thorough discussion of genius, see Andrew Gemant, *The Nature of Genius* (Springfield, Illinois: Charles C. Thomas, 1961).

Selections from Craig C. Downer's Ecuadorean notebook 5/15—6/14, 1995, some revised, June, 2020:

15th May, 1995

The human, freely relating with all living kinds… this living and interrelating in freedom—is my dream… that the whole of life may emerge… together in greater perfection. Surely so. Praise God! Amen.

16th May, 1995

7:15 AM. Try to see and appreciate the good in everyone you meet… that which is good and unique… indispensable—and not a negative stereotype. Surely not, but honor the holy truth in all you think, feel, say and do.

9:38 PM. Quito: It is extraordinary / that one can almost hear / the thought of another person / and that this sense / counts both among / the most aggravating at times / at other times / among the most exquisitely beautiful / and communicative, reassuring, uplifting! Praise God! Amen.

18th May, 1995

3 AM: I hail that gently wafting breeze/ which lifts us up and away/ from all this… / unto that yet greater state/ of perfection which us awaits. / Praise God! & Hallelujah shout!

11:09 AM: Ideas can be most liberating / when they shine a bright light/ by grace of God/ upon our future becoming. / Praise God! Amen & Amen.

How beautifully ironic, how the worldly poor become the truly rich because of their concomitant inner vision & ability to appreciate all things in this world for their link to Heaven, not having been possessed by these things in the worldly way… while all the while the so-called "rich" & cloyed, those who have that which the world has to offer, lose touch with worldly life's true meaning, ever bequeathed from On High [and precisely because of its relation as an effect thereof]. And what ever-so-free poetic justice there is in all of this!

2:30 PM: I had a brilliant idea / about *all the ideas* / that all the various / entities do form / about and around / any given subject or object / and how this exerts / its influence / in a magical way, / all according to / the Universal Sway!

There is a sense of structure… of interrelation in life and world / represented in the so-called "physical," / and that is symbol / for a Heavenly structure—most amazing! Praise God! Amen & Amen.

Surely, I am of such faith, as to know that each / particular perspective on life / experienced by each particular being / as all of us in general / manifests a special / lesson to each and all / of us, from the One who cares and dwells Above. / Praise God!

So much of all true appreciation, even in this life and world, goes on in that spiritual [*ghostly* originally used] yet enlightened realm / of spirit—does it not? / And I am happy in life when / I walk forth in blessed freedom / unbeholden to all worldly ways / or that called society / when it has become just all too worldly, / for true to myself… / true to all… / true to God. Praise God!

19th May, 1995

7:10 AM, Quito. High overcast. What great and powerful magic / there is in thoughts and feelings / by which one can / attune oneself to the / more universal order / and emerge—/ out of darkness and into light / according to God's / whole and perfect will.

To conceive life as a whole, as united and integral… no individual being excluded, nor any kinds, is a great and blessed way of conceiving life… thus, to take the Whole of Life into consideration. Praise God! Amen.

To possess that enhanced inner perspective on life / which transcends the immediate / and the temporal / is a great blessing and relief, indeed, / from worldly delusion and its / consequent spiritual darkness. Truly it is so. Praise God and shout Hallelujah!

I hail the *work of the soul* / which is of each soul / and which eternal is, / yet, which the worldly order / seldom recognizes.

20th May, 1995

3:03 AM. Quito: It is to be considered: / how all the various life situations, / that all the various individuals / do come to know, / constitute lessons arranged by Heaven / to lead us forth / out of the Darkness of the Fall / and unto the Light that restores / All this Life and our Salvation is! Praise God!

Be ye single-pointed in life / with one supreme focus / that is uplifted / and, in turn, uplifts / that honors God / and the god:/ the true nature / in each and every one. / Praise God! Amen.

Why are some people / left all alone in life / and unpopular… / left to their own company? / Could it not be / that, thereby, the Almighty / hand of providence / teaches them the better to appreciate / themselves individually / and to stand up / for those unique gifts and insights—/ those truths which God / through all Time and Experience / has uniquely given unto / each inter-complementing one? / Praise God! Amen.

There is basic / to this sensation called life / a sense of the ideal… / of that which draws us forth / unto that most cherished fulfillment—/ the ideal which we / by some most subtle / Heavenly sense do know / will surely yet realized be… / and its dawning / unveils itself / with every new tomorrow.

To possess a grander perspective in Time, / one not limited to this one life alone, / is such great blessing, / such fine / liberation, / even as is one's ability / to cherish one's Heavenly gifts, / one's every thought and feeling, / and even All that which / in this life and world / has come one's way. / Praise God! Forever and ever!

Life is—oh so very subtle… / if we will only recognize / its more refined points / rather than be taken in / by the superficial and the sham—if we only can. / For 't is a question / of attunement / to those higher / finer, all-governing planes—/ that ever to the very Highest onward leads! / Surely so such attunement does. Praise God!

Each one must / be about his or her / own special way / in life—which to identify / by grace of God / surely very lifeline is!

In some lives it is necessary to learn to value one's very aloneness for its virtuous freedom from worldly attachment—and the great stage this allows for God's higher lessons upon the consciousness to dawn!… 'T is a question of learning to see life from a higher perspective… in relation to the Greater Whole.

Worldly desire spells moral death, but in the heart's confession of sin and purification, in its uplifted living prayer, its song to Heaven, all is made well with a life… all is made to shine so bright! Praise God! and Hallelujah! shout.

22nd May, 1995

Thoughts arising while early morning bathing in El Salado mineral springs, upper Baños, Tungurahua, Ecuador (my home there for years).

(1) In as much as one can detach one's thoughts and feelings from the vulgar, worldly plane, so one is enabled to rise to that higher realization which is of Heaven. Then how marvelously one's life is transformed!

(2) In life, we must stress the Good & True & Beautiful… ever be offering that which is right, not dwelling on the negative or imperfect, for, thus, we do soar above all that is vulgar and demeaning and draw nearer to the very Kingdom of Heaven. Praise God! Amen.

(3) There come times when one realizes just how true and fine and pure are life's true goals and from what great depths of association in Time and ever concomitant Experience are drawn one's preparations and to what yet greater heights each soul does aspire!

(4) When the perverse and worldly will of life to subjugate itself to material false idols is overcome through genuine repentance and God's holy will is recognized and obeyed as pertains to one's true, unique and indispensable purpose in life, then how wondrously this life and world find itself transformed. Truly so. Praise God! Amen.

(5) There is for each given time / a special spark of Divine / accomplishment… / and those times / to carry this spark forth. / Surely so. Praise God!

(6) Learn to appreciate even the simplest aspects of life and to recognize their source in the Divine Ideal and their role in the Divine discovery, or becoming; and be not given to worldly fetish, futility and profanation of life, / but give Glory unto God On High / in all that you think, do, or say. / Praise God! I say, Praise God! Forever and ever!

(7) One learns to sense / in the very forward advance / of time / a great wonder and therefrom / derive a renewal / of what one recognizes as very home and even precious love.

(8) As we dare to be different and to separate ourselves from the mundane mentality, fixated upon externalities as it is, so we grow in wisdom and in strength before the Lord and so does all this we call "society" likewise grow.

(9) Though we are all in essence spirits, today's, as any given time's, worldly fixated society disowns this brilliant truth, preferring to subject all of life, including its own conception thereof, to the external, the vulgar and the profane. Surely this is in the very perverse nature of sin—which is Lie! To recognize this and to repent and turn once again to that ever Higher Shinning Light of Greater Truth being revealed, verily, is to Live! Praise God!

(10) Know me not merely for this body, for this life—which so fleeting was—but rather for that fine, bright spirit, which ever onward went and still yet goeth forth… back from the Fall and unto the Source—Oh! Great Discovery—So very wondrous!

(11) That blessed experience of true happiness arises within when one again realizes: *I am immortal!*

Earth Day 1995. Visit to my beautiful friends Margoth Cisneros & her precious little daughter Silvia in Baños in their humble but charming home & store in which a weeping statue of the Virgin Maria lives.

To be content in one's inmost spirit, thus, to appreciate that fine knitting which goes on, even with every succeeding moment, and that toward which this knitting tends—aye!—surely such great blessing is!

I welcome *the newness* in each succeeding moment… that which God subtly brings to all spirits… and which furthers our course back to Perfection. Praise God! Amen.

It sometimes pays / to sit down and appraise / just who calls out to one / in most endearing ways… / and, so, along these lines of sympathy / to pursue one's contacts and relations / and where they / lead on. Praise God! Amen.

I celebrate the newness of each moment as well as its indispensable connection with all that has been and, yet, shall be. Praise God! And set me free!

Sol de Los Andes Restaurant, Baños. Sunset, evening tide. It is possible for the mind and heart/ to reach such a sharp / state of focus and intention / that through whatever means / or media of communication—/ or through none—/ somehow this communicates itself / to All who one surrounds!

24th May, 1995

Ca. 10 AM. Baños. To discern the *universal pulsation* allows one to consider the unity of motion among all spirits and how forth out of Darkness and into Light we most surely go!

11:58 AM. There are those who kill life by their immorality more certainly than if they plunged a sword through its heart… and it is mainly of their <u>own</u> life of which I speak… yet because we are all inextricably related, this affects us all.

Learn to value your own personal spiritual progress and to know that it is of universal import; know that it is a window unto the same in all seemingly separate individual beings, for truly *in Spirit we are all One*… united within the Spiritual Dimension, as the very origin of the word "individual" reveals (Latin for "not divisible").

To behold and be inspired by ever new and revealing Beauty is one with the source of our continued will to live itself, the true "bread of life" that descends from Heaven. Praise God! Amen.

9:25 AM. Riobamba. Attuned to the universal spiritual essence, each new moment in life affords new wonder and makes one's face to shine so brightly. Praise God! Amen.

It is precisely from that supreme sense of irony, which stems from the as-yet-unspoken, unexpressed whole—that part as yet unknown and unannounced, unmanifest (since the Fall), that there arises that special twinkle in the eye, that special rich sense of humor, that special future-seeing faith and *elan vital* that, by the grace of God, keeps us all onward bound — verily to victory!

One thing is merely to list, cheek by jowl, the species or the elements of an ecosystem, another thing entirely it is to relate them in a fine and artful, wisely judicious and comprehensive manner, one that also looks to the great beyond, the True Source and that relates to *the Essence*.

6:03 PM. Alao village, Chimborazo, Sangay National Park office where I often stayed. An enigma: To trace the life of any spirit is to live it, to experience it (is it not?)! Yet, remarkably, we all do share in the lives of one another, even as each one does individually go forth, seemingly upon his/her/its own separate path.

26th May, 1995

5:07 AM. On expedition to El Placer in Sangay National Park today. The mystery of love counts among the most profound life has to afford… also among the most revealing. Truly so. Praise God! Amen.

To retain a high concept of life—this is most important! And could we but pierce the veil of worldly life—oh! what great wonder, meaning and promise then the Greater Eternal Life, which subsumes all our worldly lives and deaths, would hold in store for our conscious awakening. Truly so. Praise God! Amen.

8 AM. I am convinced that—to wit: and as concerns each spirit, in as much as he/she thinks and feels so he/she acts and upon the more subtle planes exerts his/her influence.

27th May, 1995

El Placer, Amazon side of Andes north of Sangay Volcano. Doing my Mountain Tapir study.

11:33 AM: As I consider: each individual is conscious and, as such, partakes of the great universal and transcendent dimension. And it is herein, in this great so-called "beyond," that life is synthesized in the finest manner… that the experience of each and every living soul in this our life and world sublimates, and transmutes such… distills such into its pure, fine essence…. And I find in the very definition of any individual life a tell-tale evidence of this great and intricate creativity… this transcendent spirit who is most surely one with all life's very essence… that living essence… more than just the body alone with its chemicals, for transcendent—most wonderful and great! Praise God!

2 PM: To know thought purely… the living reality… the ideal… is both great salvation and great joy. Truly so. Praise God! "Amen."

4:05 PM: El Placer. A great transcendent thought: A brilliant idea just occurred to me: that those great legends, myths and rituals a people develop and express over the generations do in truth individually live… indeed, even as we all individually live.… Consider now just how each life, seen from the eternal perspective, is like that vast and seemingly slow progression of the gods—which spirit-gods are verily we ourselves… the ever-existent beings inhabiting the universe and in some special fashion indispensably making it go.

4:44 PM. El Placer. Tracking Mountain Tapirs. *Tashpo* is Puruhaes word for "Fire".

Learn to have faith in everyone, for this is one's true test of universal intelligence—not how many people you can "see through" and, so, "lose faith in". For how much or how little one sees in life depends on his/her degree of spiritual enlightenment. (Thick mists coincidently lifted.)

…To appreciate the soul of life is to be ever filled with wonder and admiration for each and every being you meet.

28th May, 1995

4:25 AM. El Placer: The human voice can work wonders. So can any voice of any kind. It is a sign of the spirit… an expression. When uplifted, what a wonderful comforter it is. Praise God!

Dreamt of my folks (parents), sister, of visiting a new subdivision, of living in a high rise. The time was in the future and the place: Reno, Nevada. I sensed a strange, unprecedented ethos, one of our good Earth even more overrun with people than it already is.

8 AM. The very awareness of eternal life is great joy and the deliverance from worldly lie and sinful degradation. Surely so. Praise God! Amen. Amen.… And the contemplation of past and future lives in this expanded awareness leads to yet further, great and soul-fulfilling discoveries, indeed.

In life, it is our constant challenge of consciousness to regain whole truth. Thus, we are ever embarked upon a process that flows forth out of darkness and into light, restoring all by grace of God. This most fascinates me concerning all this life and life's stage: the world… this world… any world… all worlds… and as concerns all the multitudinous and multifarious life forms and states of consciousness and expression, for surely all are *One in Spirit*. Praise God! Amen.

9:38 AM. In the skies, in the clouds on high—aye!—what great marvels communicated are!

10:00 AM. Inspired thought concerning life: Each spirit's right to communicate with the higher spiritual realms, meaning, ultimately, with the Divine Source, is inalienable. This communion occurs at all times and is with *the true source* of life's continuance. It is especially to be noted in dreams and meditations, rhapsodies and inspired spells. It is the true life! All else taken apart from this is but… a dragging down and an obscuring of the whole being.—Know this, oh my soul, and be free from all worldly lie. Praise God! and Hallelujah! shout.

10:38 AM. Tres Gracias Cascada, Rio Palora. Misty. Birds singing. Fools leap to condemn that or whom they do not understand, but the wise seek both to learn from and to teach each unique and universal soul with whom they come into contact, as with all… and to recognize… *the great meantness* in each such meeting. Surely so. Praise God!

Yellow-beaked Fruit Jay observed in association with radio-collared tapir "Ninfa" near Rio Palora. How in each seeming separate thing can be seen all other such things by dint of their relation! This constitutes one of the great and captivating wonders of all life and world: that all things are symbols for beings, spirits all, and that we are all interrelated and ever linked at the highest causative plane that transcends over the mere world of things, or externalities. And this is such great cause for rejoicing. Praise God! Amen.

When one leaps up to a level of perception whereby all that presents itself in externalized life and world is recognized as symbol for and effect… of a higher spiritual realm… of reality and causation, then how bright life becomes, how full of meaning, truly progressive, full of promise, beautiful and serene. Truly so. Praise God! Amen.

11:30 am. Beauty is perception of the spirit. It restores the abiding consciousness of life unto its true self. It relinks the fallen soul with the ideal. Beauty is the very Heavenly food of life. It nourishes by giving meaning and purpose, sense of fulfillment and duration. Surely so. Praise God! Amen.

Some people are just bent on chopping out what they can "get" from life. They have no sense of wrong or right, or so it seems. They are dead of conscience. All they seem to care for is their worldly selves: and hedonistic pleasure is their measure of success. Little do they realize that the way they have chosen to relate and live is a sure ticket to the place of darkness and torment… to the dark, gloomy shades of Hades and, when their karmic burden becomes enormous, to the burning fires of hell for their much-needed purification! But, don't worry, the latter are not forever. For each soul is ever allowed to repent and to reascend.

In marking the sheer, subtle passage of time, something that is more than just the external events which Time enfolds, we souls can climb to a higher plane of realization… reverse the Fall and know that special magic that is in all this life and world. For truly it is ever over one and united in each and, remarkably, in all instants of Time—oh! Great Continuum! Praise God! Amen and Amen.

Possibly Illustrate this very fine poem entitled: *Who Was I?*

Rushes by edge of stream, / old friends of mine / from this and past lifetimes! / I even remember when / in bulrushes I was hid—/ Oh! Infant cradled / in ancient Egypt / then floated / upon Nile's serene / and mysterious waters… / as in very Time's… / left adrift / to some fate as yet unknown—/ Oh! Life's great adventure / and promise yet to discover! / Praise God! Forever and ever!

Learning to correctly read life and world according to many diverse and subtle signs is a most rewarding talent—and this we each must learn!

Too many people today have the screwy misconception they / must force their expression upon all others to be successful. / Realize they not / that even as they think and feel and will / within the higher, more subtle dimension / that such is communicated to all? / For truly it is so. Praise God! /… Within the realm of thought can be found such sweet and Heavenly conception—and most brilliant realization, even when one dwells in this manifest worldly plane and which dwelling / is not the only life there is!

*Very touching true story… it would be good to illustrate… this passage with photo of a trout.

Turning out to be a nice afternoon with clouds clearing and bright sun peeping through… like very God! My thoughts now turn to fishing. Francisco just caught a beautiful little 7" rainbow trout, which I photographed. But it was hard to watch this poor fish in its death throes, struggling to live and to see it killed with a stone… to "put it out of its misery." Thus, to see such an exquisite creature… such a graceful form and manifestation of the universal spirit within… beyond, brought to its seeming end in this world we shared as home.—Surely there is more to life than just its brief and fleeting manifest existence here! Surely there is a Heaven for this fish… for all creatures: a place where their spirit dwells and wherein lies their true and ever-abiding power and cause… something beyond just this Earthly destructible body, taken in and of itself.

There is a language of the heart and spirit that the worldly and efficacious minds loathe, yet, which speaks a greater, vaster, deeper, and loftier truth. Truly so there is. Praise God!

* (So special) For those who in fish see only flesh and not spirit, likewise for those who in any living kind see only what's there to be gained for man's worldly estate, both life and world's an empty hellish place, indeed, wherein they themselves do defile in the most thoughtless, disgusting manner! But for those who can relate to *the spirit* that quickens all flesh, this world is more than just this living flesh, this living world—for all its dreadful suffering and woes—is still a place of glowing promise and of hope, wherein God's holy mandate is and will be more fully fulfilled, as magical Time progresseth. Praise God!

I find that the listening to my own true thoughts and feelings is a lot more enlightening than simply being drawn in and hypnotized by the world out there, by the mere external and what others want of me—for how dreadfully un-whole and unholy this is… this fallen, externally fixated society where the holy spirit of life is subjugated to that which is less than its true and holy, for whole, self.

3:30 PM. La Playa, Rio Palora. As I continue to track mountain tapirs, especially Ninfa, this profound thought occurs to me:

The sinful, profane, worldly mind tries to make everything concrete… manipulatable by worldly means. This is the way of folly, of death and to hell. But the uplifted mind and heart is not so profane, but all perceives in relation to and as stemming from the Holy Spirit… ultimately from God… the True Source. And a resurrected mind-heart-will performs great wonders, even in this life and world, truly bringing Heaven to Earth. Praise God! I say, Praise God! and Hallelujah! shout.

29th May, 1995

Still at El Placer, P.N. Sangay. Tracking Mountain Tapirs all day.

4:16 PM. Laguna Negra Pass, Parque Nacional Sangay, returning to Alao.

Life is full of birth / Life is full of death. / And there's a going in / and out by many souls / through many diverse gates—/ Oh! Wondrous Life!… / But ever it is in Holy Spirit—/ that Kingdom Within / that we have our fine, true home. / Praise God! Amen.

5:32 PM. Alao Station P.N. Sangay: Dreams are adjusters / of our universal relationships. / They involve / our evolving consciousness / of whole and holy truth… / our reversing of the Fall. / They tell / us of our greater self, / in relation to each and all / other immortal spirits. / Oh! Wondrous dreams! Praise God!

30ᵗʰ May, 1995

6:03 AM. Alao. P.N. Sangay Station.

I hail the individual conscious being, eternal and immortal, that spark of the Divine, which in all ways ever returneth home unto the Source, all possibilities exploreth, in all ways rediscovereth All Glorious Truth, and has been doing this ever since the Fall—all to the Great and Everlasting Glory of God!

Heaven shows forth its supreme gifts in the most subtle of ways, unprescribed by worldly means, to that humble and contrite heart who confesses sin and opens itself up, like a leaf or a flower, to receive the blessings from On High. Seen this way, all of life is a rising up to receive Heaven's greater blessing.—This the very humble plants and trees do teach us, as they rise up from the Earth's soil to receive the Sun's light and blessing. Truly there is a most profound symbology in all of this—and all spirits, all consciousness, are together in this upward rise… out of Darkness and into Light. Truly so. Praise God!

Be appreciative of the most common and everyday in life and world… for it is grand and each facet is unique yet complements the whole. Take nothing for granted, oh my soul. Praise God! Hallelujah!

Learn to celebrate life in and of and for Spirit, for this is to know the Truth and not be bound by worldly misconceptions, false idolatries and lies. Surely so. Praise God!

31ˢᵗ May, 1995

Thoughts at El Salado thermal baths I entered ca. 5 AM for fresh water. Lies near foot of mighty Volcan Tungurahua, which I summitted. Later this exploded and many were killed or… fled, but the town of Baños was spared.

We must learn to say, as did the Christ: 'Stand behind me, Satan' as we each go forth out of darkness and into Light, the Living Light of our Salvation. Praise God! Amen & Amen… Now, concerning death, that death which each one of us must face, who lives in the body: it is a necessary relinquishment of attachment. For each one must die to his/her worldly attachments in order to be reconciled with his/her greater, purer home… that eternal abode of all spirits… that spiritual dimension… that wondrous and all-embracing Heaven. Surely it is so… and I ever look forward to the new and dawning day. Praise God! Forever and ever!

3:20 PM (very special message.): Of great value and remark is that ability, that great gift, to connect… one moment with another… one experience with another—even those most distant and most far, remote and seemingly disparate, yet ever connected by such a fine and subtle thread. Praise God!

4:40 PM. The life of the heart need not be a dirty life, for liberated from sinful attachment, this can prove the very means of such wondrous rise… every by grace and power of God…. Free of possessive individual attachments, one can rise to such beautiful heights… soar on the wings of a more universal identity… aiding others and, in turn, being so aided when in need… fulfilling God's holy plan. Truly so life can be for you and for me. Praise God! Amen.

1ˢᵗ June, 1995

6:27 AM. En route in bus from Baños to Quito. Thoughts:

Sin is life's tragedy… overcoming sin and realization of Virtue is life's victory. Praise God!… Learn to recognize, oh my soul, all the trappings of temptation, in this life and world… those that call to the fallen, sinful self, for these are only darkness and delusion, lies that call to moral death. —Beware of this and go not the way of the profane and vulgar. But, rather, honor the Lord God and rebuke all such foolishness. Be a Light shining unto Darkness, a splendid example of the way back from the Fall, restoring all. And let your standard be with God and not with those who idolize the mere externalities of the world and of life in it. Arise and Go Forth to Victory, oh my soul, whomsoever ye be!

7:29 AM. Ambato en route Quito. As in all creatures, strange or familiar, big or small, it's their undying spirit that unites them… and us all. Surely so. Praise God!

3ʳᵈ June, 1995

7:08 AM. Tumbaco, near Quito. Learn in life, oh my soul, that the essence is not beholden or dependent upon the mere appearance… that all that is merely manifest, or external, including all the physical, is effect… caused, not cause, and that the great cause lies within… each and every one. Praise God! Amen.

4ᵗʰ June, 1995

Never ye fear, oh my soul, for all is preserved in spirit… All that has ever existed either in space or in time is perfectly preserved in essence therein, for Spirit is the True Cause. So, follow no lesser idols and remember that the words people speak or write or record are but mere inklings of that great and complete truth that lies within.

The outward forms and situations of all this we call "life and world" seem to change, but change not the whole and holy truth thereof concerning… that truth which is the immortal soul, the Spark Divine… and God's rediscovery, God's glorification is in all ways wrought.

When will vain pretentious people learn that there's more to life in terms of intrinsic value and worth than just what he/she can exploit or consume or use in some worldly way? When will we learn that there's soul expressing through all the manifest forms and that this soul is universal and one with his own and that its very recognition as to its own essential purpose and appointment from

God in Heaven is all but enough reason for its being here with us and for our being here with it? For together we do surely go forth. And, surely, this is according to God's most perfect will. Praise God!

Be honest and true with your brother / sister / whatever relative / neighbor, etc., honoring his / her / its unique soul, role, path, place — and all shall go well into your future…

10:37 AM. Tumbaco. I perceive the subtle manner in which language works to involve souls in a system of assumptions, of rigid forms of relation, thus, to force upon the individual some state or condition for life that is lesser than its true place, role, heritage bequeathed by the Universal and the Divine. Praise God! Amen.

Thought on knowing different languages: it is wise to be aware both of the virtue and the vice in each language and, thus, through knowing more than just one, by means of greater contrast, one is enabled to rise to a higher, purer expression of Truth itself… ultimately the very language of God.

Creer es Poder is Spanish for "To Believe is To Be Able to Do", Spanish expression given me by my friend Ondina Landazuri of Tumbaco.

12:57 PM. Thought awaiting at Quito bus station to return to Baños, 3-hour trip, lovely volcanoes:

This I note having lived in this lifetime in a few different cultures, as over many lifetimes in many others: that in each culture there is a certain way of confronting life that presents itself… a certain rhythm and attitude and that this bears direct relation to music… that magical, living music ever being composed and going forth in each and every one of us. Complementing one another over time, all such cultures evolve and interblend, ever rising yet higher to our most noble end. Truly so. Praise God! Amen.

3:10 PM. Of such great value it is to note that in the mind-and-heart's pure upliftment is very Heaven brought to Earth. Failing this, the converse brings disharmony, discord, and hellish conditions.… Yet, in the great fulness of time, these obstacles, each and all, shall be overcome. For such is our blessed destiny. Praise God! Hallelujah!

A beautiful affirmation in this equally beautiful poem:

And I wandered / like some disembodied spirit / in this world / unattached / dreaming dreams / conceiving such precious meanings / as only Heaven can bestow / unto the upturned soul!

Not to take for granted any single experience or encounter, aye, 't is the way to certain restoration… of all full balance and proportion… therein to discern Heaven's full lesson. Truly it is so. Praise God! Amen.

5th June, 1995

10:54 AM. Quito. Sucre International Airport awaiting flight back to U.S. Uplifted thought:

I love to recognize life's pure, fine essence / thus, not to be hung up / on the superficialities / and the externalities / but to recognize / the living presence / and by so recognizing / this living presence / to be uplifted / unto the consciousness / of all life's spiritual unity /… and by "life" I mean to say / *all who exist* / in not just a body / in the here and now / in this life and in this world / but *all beings who exist* / purely and in their own right / and in indispensable relation to ALL. / Praise God! and shout Hallelujah!

9th June, 1995

Back home in Nevada.

Each being must continue along those themes for and to which all his/her/its past experience and inspirations do call. Be true to yourself and be on!

To recognize and appreciate the soul of life wherever, whenever and in whatever form it may raise its head and to do so with highest art and attunement, beyond all mere materialist monuments and idols and the demagogues who employ these to suppress and manipulate others, in this life and in this world, truly such fine victory is! And this fine inner art shall make this our life and this our world—and life of all lives and world of all worlds—every so fine someday…. Such constitutes a heavenly mandate that won't end until accomplished… as is written in the very stars themselves! Praise God! Amen.

Do not overlook the power and the importance of thought, for 't is surely great. Thought advances toward whole and holy truth: its true nature. The Fall brought this motion about, that we may all rediscover truth and in doing so glorify God, each uniquely, yet all together. Praise God! Forever & ever.

10th June, 1995

9:05 AM. Those who turn their back on God, do thereby cast themselves into outer darkness. It is they who have closed the door unto their very salvation as far as any one life is concerned. This is a warning, yet, though one seems to fail, yet shall he/she be given another chance, for such is the Kingdom of Heaven.

Regard all whom you meet as one in universal spirit and your meeting them as right and meant—one with the universal plan.

Life is a struggle between sin and virtue, lie and truth, darkness and light. And this struggle is primarily an individual one. Those who deny it are often overtaken by the perverse forces of darkness and sin. Those who recognize it and who seek God's help are very much uplifted… suffused with a miraculous living light that sees them through and over all difficulties. Surely so. Praise God!

Know that you are one with all that is… an indispensable integral… and that what you are and what you do can never be forgotten, no matter by whom. Surely it is so and surely you shall make a difference. Be not deceived by superficial worldly put downs, which are not lighted by universal love, but represent only the sinful fallen state… that which is to be overcome. Praise God! Amen.

Concentrate upon life's positive aspects; honor its spirit, that of each individual. Be not drawn into worldly delusion… false idolatry of the mere external aspects of life. But, rather, serve and worship God in spirit and in truth… that you may be saved! Give praise to the Lord God on High!

There is magic in words to those who enter their soul and spiritual origin. Words go concomitantly with each soul's universal journey of enlightenment… of Truth's rediscovery. Words are like a higher plane of reality, a closer link with Spirit, symbolizing all that surrounds us hereabout in this life and in this world, be this composed of sticks, stones or the very bodies, plant and animal, that enclose us spirits all who herein from time to time find abode. Surely so it is. Praise God!

One's moral success or failure is explicitly written in one's whole physiognomy and manner as manifest in this life and world. But take heart, for just as the root of that which is wrong rests with the individual spirit and its identity, so the root of one's salvation lies likewise in and with the individual spirit's capacity to reform, to confess sin and to honor and, so, thereby receive blessings from the Lord God On High.

I hail all the various life forms as manifestations of Heaven, of the spirit world. So perfect are they! So various and unique! Surely to God they do attest… to the Master of the Universe… not to mere externality and physicality taken in and of itself, like some false idol, like some satanic lie. Be not so taken in, so by fallen self "deluded", but give glory to God on High.

Enter into life in grand style, oh my soul! Be not dismayed. Trust in Heaven's grace, for all here below most beautiful shall be made—if only you will *believe*. Truly so. Praise God!

Seek virtue and the pleasing of God in this life and world… the pleasing of God above all else… that your life shall be an honor and not a disgrace… as judged by those standards that are universal and true. And may God help us all in this.

11:29 AM. Each knows that truth which his/her heart and mind and will have to realize and express and only he/she can realize and express it and knows how. Be not confused on this point by others who would monopolize your life for their own selfish aggrandizement. For this is not the way of true understanding and love. Surely not. Praise God!

Each life is like a musical composition, in truth is a living musical composition whose theme at first after birth waxes then reaches a climax at maturity then wanes, subsiding unto death. But the immortal hope, the Heavenly instilled vision, lives on with the spirit! And this: inasmuch as it is linked with all that is true and holy, shall never die… and shall most surely prevail in the end. Truly it is so. Praise God! Amen.

To the spiritually enlightened, all this life and world becomes a great wonder and marvel, for its link to Heaven is recognized; by vision of faith, its ultimate perfection and glorification of God is known. So be ye strong of mind and of heart, oh my soul. Shout Hallelujah!

Vulgar passion leads to a life of rashness and "de-virtue-ing"… debasement… the enslavement of the higher self to vice. This is detestable sin… the Devil's work… the Devil's lie! Surely, truly none of this shall stand the Light of Day!

There is nothing more fascinating than a soul. It is greater than all the mere physical universe put together. Indeed, it is more than this. Praise God!

Truly great writing proceeds from an exactness of expression, a faithfulness to Whole Truth, including especially the spiritual aspect, for this is of the essence.

9:05 PM. Look beyond the merely manifest for your source in life of joy and inner resurrection, for each moment is an unprecedented, unique advance… a reversal of the Fall to Sin… a resurrection within… within the spiritual dimension, which we all do share. Of this, be ever so aware… rejoicing in God's ever greater revelation… And look beyond mere things, for it is that living presence of which you are integral that matters most… that sacred communication with the universal God.

Virtue's way is always the greatest… that of vice, however adulated by worldly society, is the way of failure, for righteous Heaven, God above, is the true judge. And when we ourselves attune to this higher plane, though dwelling alone—how high and perfect sing our hearts, our minds, our wills… together still… uplifted in songs whose pure themes Universal—Eternal are!

11ᵗʰ June, 1995

7 AM. Moral turpitude is life's true failure, but moral rectitude and uplifted faith and belief is all things restored… all things, I say, meaning all Heavenly ideals… those living aspects of the whole self that call each of us back to our true nature—back to God!

Learn to perceive life in all its diverse and intricate forms as the Heavenly hand of spirit expressing itself in all its possibilities, yet all as one and in united form when perceived from the highest plane.… Remain not of fallen mind and heart, but perceive the sacred essence. Surely so do and in your uplifted, attuned belief, honor God on High!

Each life form has its corresponding ideal, each individual: its unique insight and role. All are interdependent. None is apart. All go forth in God's sight, perfectly, however it may seem to the contrary, for the perfect and universal laws, the high moral standards, the rules of harmony and attunement, of aesthetics and true beauty, of cause and effect, apply throughout the whole. Praise God!

9:04 A.M. Spiritually each one of us can best and in highest manner ourself attune, rather than merely by means of the physical body or any or all things that are merely physical, taken apart from the spiritual. Yet, attuned, believing in the spiritual, one can divine the true cause for all things physical and, being of right mind and priority, summon the splendid truth residing in, yet beyond, all manifest creation and, so, honor the Lord God who ever dwelleth On High.

Learn to critically evaluate what is presented here in this world, thus, to consult your higher lights, your Heavenly link, and not be overwhelmed by any superficial situation focused strictly on externalities, for this preserves your life in all virtue and integrity. Surely so. Praise God!

By remembering higher spiritual reality concerning all fellow entities and even all objects, places and natural phenomena, and in recalling the spiritual source and cause of all this life and world, each one of us overcomes the spiritual darkness of the fall to sin and comes to reign victoriously through uplifted belief, thus, regaining God's free blessing, even as the Christ. Truly so. Praise God!

Each individual soul knows what unique gifts he/she has received from Heaven and that unique role he/she has to play in the universal scheme of our common becoming, of our returning from the fall to sin back unto the glory—and must let no other one exclusively tell him/her what to do or be… only God On High.

Sin is life's pitfall and Virtue is the way out and True Love is the key, likewise True Knowledge, Recognition of the Whole, not just the part—all this: by the grace and power of God—our Salvation is! Praise God! Amen.

We live in spirit; and it is each one's consciousness of this pure essence that liberates him/her from all the mere corporeal manifestation taken by itself apart from higher spirit.

Time is like a butterfly who flits and flies, alights here then there, but cannot be pinned down. And so it is, my friend, with the spirit, or soul, of each and every one… with all this we call life, or creation, or evolution… for we go on unto that Perfection, which, being our end, paradoxically was our beginning. —Oh, Great Mystery revealed to the inspired perception of the conscious spirit… awakening in all full light and blessing. Truly so. Praise God! Amen.

Worldly people become ensnared in their own lustful possessiveness and conceit and, thus, hooked by vice, are dragged down to the dark and tormented region, or, rather, to states of spiritual darkness known to many as Hell. Be aware and Take Care!

Money is no substitute for spiritual class, nor are expensive clothes, homes, cars, meals nor any possessions a substitute for spiritual style. For in life there is virtue and the absence of virtue, i.e. vice, and the former is as the light to the latter's darkness, the truth to a lie. Therefore, repent ye of your sins, rise up and be free. Surely nothing but the best awaits any universal soul who confesses sin and worships God in spirit and in truth. Surely so. Praise God and Hallelujah! shout.

Adopting worldly standards only leads to madness, but retaining and regaining one's links to the higher spiritual reality, or Heaven, restores soundness and blessedness in all one's life and being. Truly so. Praise God! Amen.

To rise in consciousness closer to God, which is the same as closer to Truth, is to uplift and to transform, in a positive way, all the world. Surely so. Praise God!

Language can be used perversely by benighted people to promote lies and false idols in the minds and hearts and wills of its hearers. Contrarywise, language can be used by enlightened, spiritually attuned people to uplift this life and world and all who dwell therein. Language spoken or written or sung can be a most beautiful reflection, even an expression of the Divine Source. So just take care that you do so when truly inspired by the true meaning of all such symbols. Surely so do. Praise God!

4:06 PM. How vast and beautiful are the inner vistas of the spirit… for which all this external world of space and even of time is but symbol. For the spirit is greater than either Space or that which transcends Space: Time. For Spirit contains both Space and Time, yet surges beyond. It is truly the highest dimension. And anyone's enhanced perception within Space and Time, within the realm of all possibility, which is to say, the meaning of all points upon our universal journey, back from the Fall and even before—aye! —how great, grand, liberating, indispensable and beautiful is!

The enlightened view of life perceives the inner spiritual oneness and is not divisive, but sees all as one in God, our true Source, our true origin, our true end. Surely so. Praise God! Amen & Amen.

11ᵗʰ June, 1995

Life & World & Time / is like the writing of a book / and so is Music! / With each new moment / another thought, feeling—new aspect / of the universal experience unfolds—/ comes to be known, / is written, / another note is sung… / and by each and every one! /… Now, nothing is every lost, / not one moment… / not one word, note, or impression / however subtle. / And to those so loftily attuned, / it is surely possible / to read this whole book /… that book which is written / by each individual soul / throughout the universe of Time—/ and, remarkably, by all of us as one… / within the Great Eternal Spirit… / that which never ends. / Truly it is so. Praise God! Amen.

As the soul rises, its thoughts progress from the mere recognition of externalities taken separately, to the recognition of the spiritual essence itself.

18:41 hours. Each individual being traces a unique path forth in life, as in so-called death (which is, in fact, but a transition within the greater life). And this unique path truly accomplishes each soul's unique yet universally and indispensably related eternal progress. Thus, in the ultimate analysis, no one and no one's life, or path, is without redeeming value. Remarkably, as our paths do coincide, we all together weave that great, by-God-inspired Tapestry of Life—most amazing to behold, for made in the very image and likeness of God!

People get into such a rut in their relationships. They forget how to express their true thoughts and feelings. Yet, this cannot last, for what greater gift has anyone to give to his or her fellow spirit? Be genuine! Be true! Express your genuine message uplifted to the On High! Be not motivated by the perverse and iniquitous tendency to lie, which is the temptation to sin, for nothing good can come of this!… For all that comes to pass in life must be seen as leading back to and glorifying God. All that does not do such but makes worldly fetish of its fallen state is doomed to utter confounding and failure!… Yet, even from these hard lessons ultimately Salvation Springs!

Go ye ahead to every sure, true and noble goal; be ye not taken in by worldly false idols, however puffed up or sugared over or seemingly popular, for in the latter is only death and delusion, but true life and the fullness thereof is to be found in the Kingdom Within and with God! And this makes all things bright, for perceived in relation to their true cause!

The great mystery of life is the life of the individual conscious being. Facing this mystery, which is in each and every one of us, a light supernal shall, by the grace of God, dawn upon the consciousness and concerning the consciousness, that the whole truth shall be known and the victory be God's in each and every being!

Whenever anyone of us puts down any fellow soul, no matter how humble or great his/her/its body and earthly abode, most of all we do damage to our very own selves, not the one we seek to disparage, deny and even to do away with. Think about this! And remember also how important it is not to put down yourself.

To perceive the immortal life of the individual, including, of course, one's very own self, is to clear away much confusion and blockage and to allow such a greater and fuller understanding of life to shine through in all its great promise and glory.

What supreme art there is in a flower, an orchid, an iris, a snail, an exquisite, streamlined fish… whatever… for it is the supreme art of God, bound with purpose, intimately bound with spirit, that each individual presence expresses.

Anyone whose consciousness blossoms in the living light of Divine Knowledge comes to shine with a supernal beauty and perfection, even in this life and in this world. Surely so. Praise God!

To give the glory to God in all that is merely of this life and world—this most important is! Failing this, all worldly endeavors fail, for they become mere false idols, lies and misconceptions, which drag one down to Hell…. Surely there is a better way. Dear Lord God, grant us the faith to rise above.

Any lying, mocking, sinful, worldly society is no true judge, or arbiter, of life's true meaning and worth, however it may arrogantly claim to be. But in higher spiritual attunement, one realizes Heaven, for God in Heaven knows and appreciates each and every living spirit and provides for this one—even oneself… for such is the Majesty of Heaven. Praise God! Amen and Amen.

The Devil hates rebuke, like a hot coal seems to hate water. Even so is every unrepentant sinner in relation to the holy one of God… his/her uplifted heart and mind, his/her inspired words. But to the faithful belongs life's true and ultimate victory. Truly so, as the holy spirit bears witness. Praise God!

13:54 hours. A society that treats money with more respect than souls… that is blind to the universal spiritual laws of justice and morality and recognizes only physical bodies and the physical possession thereof in the worldly sense—such is a society whose relations come more to resemble Hell than Heaven, for their perverse worship is filled with falsehoods, twisted assertions and outright shameless lies! Sternly these perverse and abominable ones shall be judged!

14:21 hours. Those who serve Mammon and the base wants of human society, go out in disgrace from this life and world, but those who serve Heaven's high calling, life's true purpose, know honor and true reward from the Source of all this manifest life and world. Truly so. Praise God!

22:46 hours. In every individual soul is all that is fine and intelligent… strong and faithful and good. Likewise, the opposite of these, i.e. their absence in our awareness, may betimes occur… yet, ever and anon, it is the positive that prevails… and no one is to be dismissed… and ever even as we each and all proceed to live, so we unravel that very grandest of mysteries as we go on—unto that Perfection from which we sprang.

How every individual expresses a unique spirit is a fact of life that I find most wonderful, intriguing and faith-inspiring. Truly so. Praise God!

I remark with great lamentation how in this human society today the one who has most to give, who most God's precious gifts has received, is often the one most shunned, while some blabbing, superficial blowhard is given nearly all the credit and attention… he or she who posits foolishness and shallow-minded trivialities and whose motivation is mischief and perversion! Surely, truly, none of this the Light of Day shall stand!

13th June, 1995

After meditation at 7:35 AM. High cirrus clouds.

Our life is an adventure of expanding appreciation of its own true essence… a learning to divine the whole and, therefore, holy spirit… a learning to recognize all life's and all world's True Source. And here I am reminded of the great Greek philosopher Socrates' great dictum: "Know Thyself".

All things in this life and world must be seen, heard and in all ways sensed and appreciated for their spiritual source, for their essential link to Heaven—to God. For, if not, then only lies and false idols these things become in one's mind and heart, and this profanes life and makes one's own life an abomination! But the good news is that such error can quickly be corrected with… an uplifted change of heart.

8:51 AM. Those who trust in money and worldly possessions shall be utterly confounded, but those who place their trust, their faith, their belief in the universal and uplifted spirit and the eternal moral laws governing our becoming shall be most marvelously uplifted… *realized* in the fullest sense of the word… then in their very present lives they shall see such glorious fulfillment.

The pride of the flesh leads only to Hell, but the relinquishment of this fallen, sinful nature, through the love of all that is high and true and noble, leads surely to one's salvation—and ultimately to the wondrous upliftment and transformation of all this world and all the spirits who dwell herein. Praise God! I say, Praise God! Amen.

How petty, vulgar and degraded are the minds and hearts who only concentrate upon their differences with others and the means of putting themselves in a "superior" position thereover, rather than confessing their own woeful iniquity and, thus, paving the way for that vision of life which sees the wondrous spiritual oneness of all beings and how we all go forth together and remarkably back to Perfection… back to God. Truly it is so for all of us. And we are ever *one in spirit*. Praise God and Hallelujah! shout. [Especially fine fervent passage recalls: "Comparisons are odious".]

Societies and species, cultures and races, groups and groups of groups, and groups of "groups of groups," etc.—all are inextricably bound together… like a glue in a pot. Consider this: no cubit in space is separable from any other in this dimension, nor in that higher dimension which includes Space-Time. And in Time, no moment is separable from any other moment… and each moment is tripartite: past, present and future in reverse order, since first it is future (waiting to happen) then present (now happening) then past (already happened). Yet, none of Time is lost, for every single moment is inextricably united to all similar moments, past, present and future, that exist throughout the whole vast and all-inclusive Continuum of Time. And as we each and all do live, do go forth in time (and we are ever together in this great and universal journey), we each and all are discovering that ever Greater Truth, realizing that ever greater Justice, in whose Complete Discovery—that awaits us all—shall be found our true Salvation…. Therefore, I say: as in all the many places in Space and as in all the many moments in Time, so too it is in the highest dimension: Spirit that all beings shall find their completion.… It is written: "In Spirit, We are All One… and Spirit is Divine.".… All Space and what's transcendent of Space: All Time—both are derived from that higher dimension that is ever Spirit, for Spirit rises beyond both Space and Time, aka Space-Time, and is composed of the ubiquitous and living Presence… that which, or rather *who* is reality's very essence. To realize this is to escape worldly delusion. Praise God! Amen.

12:34 PM. There must be a sense of true progress, in this life and world… of making forward advance, not just more and more futile repetition. This progress comes from the sublime reality… that which stands beyond… that which is true cause, not mere manifest effect taken in and by itself. For true progress concerns a reawakening to the essential and, so, is consciously one with the Divine. This is real; let no one confuse and tell you differently on this point.

A thought unaccompanied by a feeling is an impossibility, indeed, for mind and heart are joined… and so is will.

3:23 PM. The degree to which one is bound in this worldly life, depends upon his/her degree of attachment to the external and to the prevailing status quo and to what extent such attachment is overcome and the pure and Godly spirit—*the kingdom within*—is realized and actualized through uplifted belief and consistent action and lifestyle. Truly so. Praise God! Amen.

16:16 hours. Much unjust viciousness results from the failure to comprehend those who are highly risen in spiritual realization and the consequent blind and vicious lashing out against such. Hence arise the martyrs, those who truly care enough about life here below to express and exhort all beings, however fallen, to a higher perception and way of life.

Life itself is the greatest work of art—and this includes so-called death, which is but the transition back to the greater, more inclusive eternal life. All goes forth whether manifest in this plane or not; and all beings go forth together. There is no creation, neither destruction, but all eternal is… in ultimate analysis one with God… Divine. And the process of arriving at the ultimate analysis occurs in all we call "living"… which is the regaining of truth, in ever more aware and splendid, elevated consciousness, universally attuned in Space and what's more in Time and what's most of all in Spirit. Truly it is so. Praise God!

Seek out the company, not of those who revile the Lord and all holy ones, but of those pure and humble hearts who know God and will not relinquish their hearts, minds, wills—their lives to any corrupting influence, or any worldly lie. Surely, they shall stand with honor upon the Judgement Day!

The old become the young and the young become the old, as life goes round and round, yet ever more perfect grows, as we all emerge from darkness unto light, reversing the Fall. Truly so. Praise God!

The right perception of the simple, pure existence of any individual spirit is a wonder whose sublime glory the very Heavens declare! And consider this: it is in our attitudes and penchants that we either make dismal descents into life's dark side or glorious ascents to life's higher possibilities by following the glorious "effulgence" of God's Living Light!

There is something about the realization of death that makes life a lot more earnest, for one perceives more clearly this present life's overall purpose in context of one's many lives. Praise God!

Imagine the realm of truth evoked by rightly applied words and attune yourself to the appropriate and timely inspiration from On High. Be so inspired to any worthy form of expression such commands. Aye! For such will provide a veritable gateway unto all that was, is and, yet, will be. And I have this further to say: Oh! Armchair traveler, how vast too is your reach!

I remark the futility of any mere quantitative assessment of life… how the individual being begins its entrance into its manifest life with a mere whim of desire and through the tiny, tiny seeds of its mother's and father's joining expands from the infinitesimal to a quite substantial manifest *corpus* (body)… yet, ever the essence defies mere quantification, for the spirit is qualitative, "stuff of dreams," spirit free, transcendent, of highest dimension, beyond all mere "physicality, yet at cause thereover."

Learning to appreciate the immortal soul of everyone you meet, you advance in truth and develop a right concept and expression of your own self and role in whatever manifest life and world you find yourself… And this right concept is defined by your relation to all about you. Surely so—Oh! Great mystery of life!

Thought is a very mysterious process; remarkably it automatically finds itself reflected… manifest… expressed in all this we call life and world. —Oh, great wonder!

Remarkably, those with whom we find ourselves associated are not here for no reason, but our links with these fellow souls are drawn from the deep past and reach unto the distant future.

14th June, 1995

6:26 AM. Love is a welcoming of spirits, not just into this life but, as it turns out, into future lives, for to engage in this is to call spirits into incarnation… the babies, as well as to call each other, both mother and father, to reestablish a bond that can result in their being born through each other in future lives. Yet, it is not just this fleshy business that love is most about, but rather that spiritual communication and where this leads that is most precious. Let us therefore strive to keep it at a high level and not degrade it that all may be well with our souls.

Respect that Source in your life that is sublime… that voice which still and sure does speak within the inmost recesses of your being… that beautifully haunting voice of truth which keeps you going, assuring you of all goodness and of that sacred justice which rules over all lives throughout all times…balancing all in just proportion. —Into the life of each and every spirit this voice must come… this living voice… this presence that must be felt and thought and experienced as one and united throughout all the very universe of beings… of Being. Praise God! [Special inspired passage.]

The soul in incarnate life experiences so much… so then there comes a time for reflection upon the meaning of it all and how this integrates with the whole of universal becoming. Hence, there comes maturity and a fading back away into that higher dimension from which one came, wherein all that was experienced, however difficultly countenanced at the time, perfectly integrated resumes, even as it was in the past before the Fall. Thus, each and all of us shall again restore our awakening consciousness upon the right track… embarked upon that brilliant road that leadeth home, that leadeth to Heaven, to God!

Listen to the sublime voice that speaks within. It informs you of the truth concerning all things. Be not misled by humans' false values including money, based on worldly possessiveness and whose end is destruction and Hell. Rather, recognize the true natural and their ever-linked spiritual values, those which honor the spirit in all things, places, times, fellow lives, fellow beings. Recognize the true source that onward and upward leadeth. Be sure to do so. Praise God forevermore!

Life's greatest gifts, life's greatest rewards, are those dispensed from Heaven, from God… and all one has to do is repent and sincerely desire these greater gifts in order to receive them. Praise God! Amen.

By recognizing the Heavenly reason for each event and situation—and all such are subtly related—life takes on a beautiful meaning. And one realizes that all such events and situations and relations in this manifest life tend toward the all-inclusive Supreme Goal. Praise God!

One's emotional state is absolutely critical. Remaining besmirched by sin, one cannot progress. But confessed and cleared up, atoned, one opens the very psychic gates of Heaven… unto Paradise. Truly so one does. Praise God!

10:23 AM. There comes in the life of each and every one, a time to shine, a time to form meaningful bonds, a time to progress according to one's Heavenly appointed purpose… unique and meant for "now"… for this unique and universal impingement of spiritual forces—Oh! Great wonder of life!

Learn to appreciate what Heaven has given you, oh my soul, and to bring this to full fruition. Be not mistaken and lured into false worldly standards, but be true to Heaven's calling, which is back to life's true source, for anything the lesser leads but to death, meaning a deadening of the spirit, yet though the body liveth! Think about this!

10:35 AM. Ironically, to get what you want in the worldly way of possession so often turns out to spell one's moral death, but to remain idealistic and Heaven-bound proves every great and ennobling good… thus, not to fall victim to the "world," but conquering the world, even as Christ conquered, in order to fulfill God's holy and eternal plan… life's true Victory occurring first within and vanquishing over all sin. Praise God! Amen.

A disharmonious consciousness bent on evil and destruction, non-repentant, broadcasts only hell, for such a one dwells spiritually in Hell; but the one over whom the wholesome and saving attitude of uplifted grace does shine, knows Heaven within and to all and sundry very Heaven does express, proclaim. Surely so. Praise God! Amen.

Recognize the spirit, the living essence, in animate life, and even in so-called "inanimate" world, for spirit is truth… cause… Godliness. That living presence who does not cease to exist is of the essence; and our purpose in life is to Glorify God; and, thus, it is we come to prove and reinstate the Divine in every interrelated fraction of our being… restoring harmony throughout… rediscovering the Perfect Truth in all ways, which ways are our individual lives; and these are subtly woven together throughout time. Praise God! Amen.

The process of living is a communion to the end of re-establishing the forgotten wholeness of Truth. It is a rediscovery. In this process occurs the true glorification of God, as we each and all enhance our appreciation of all that is. As we progress, there occurs an increasing, resounding victory over all un-wholeness and perverse lie. This process is universal… going on in simply all that is and all who are… this we call life… this journey forth of the living presence… seemingly apart… born to body and external limitation… yet ever subtly together… united in the highest spiritual dimension… wed in God. Surely so. Praise God! and Hallelujah! shout.

Do not fall into the trap of negativism, but rather conceive beyond what appears to be this imperfect worldly order and unto that which shall be restored… regained… as the fall to sin is reversed. Be ye adamant in this. Surely so. Praise God! and Hallelujah! shout.

This concerning life: That it is within each and every individual spirit that the crux does lie… and no one can be cast out from the universal purview of importance…. Think universally and, by this, I mean to say: Think of Spirit, for this is the highest plane… even in each and every one. Praise God! Amen.

Learn to identify your inner instinct, to be in touch with your true thoughts and feelings, for these are universally attuned. They shall not lead you astray. And there is an inner rhythm of the heart and of the mind and of the will… a melody which involves these three and which sweeps all life forth… all individual spirits… within the highest Realm of Universally Uniting Spirit. Truly so there is. Praise God!

Honor the wind that blows in Nature's World and Heaven's sweet inspiration from God; both fall to all souls and outshine all vulgar propaganda based on sinful motivation. Praise God! Amen.

Writing and Reading is like living. The spirit of consciousness is challenged to grasp that great, overall meaning and the goal of our onward becoming. So is all that flows forth… first future, then present, then past, yet all ever preserved, no stitch in time destroyed within that great and universal flow we call Experience.

There is a spirit to words, a unique *elan*, which is linked with all the universal creative powers.

Transcendence and Greater Perspective… the fruit of expanded consciousness… the Love of Whole Truth—is where all life tends, is the hallmark of all true intelligence, curiosity and emotional yearning. Praise God!

From recognizing the virtue that exists between valid opposites, true growth and greater appreciation of all this we call "Life and World" does in synthesis spring.

He/she who recognizes the inner spark… immortal soul… the spirit of each one… sees through all apparent worldly compromise and degradation. Such a one knows how to honor the eternal… even in a plant or animal… and this attainment counts among life's truest treasures. Praise God! Forever.

Sin will never work, so don't kid yourself. It is always degrading. To abstain from sinful ways is to gain true victory in life. All who maintain otherwise only kid themselves and you—or just plain lie!

That which one puts together in life is one's very redemption… every by the Grace of God.… And the being of each life is given a certain special impetus to accomplish its Heavenly appointed ends… and overall end. Praise God! Amen.

Where one goes in life depends upon which aspects of reality one appreciates. Yet, surely, no lop-sidedness shall be tolerated in our progression, but all shall be restored in wholesome balance… "some fine day" all join in Perfection. So be ye of good faith and jump for joy!

Worldly vanity is the beginning of moral downfall… and one's downfall in all ways, but in love of truth and the contrite spirit of repentance, is all true virtue and proportion and blessing restored. Praise God!

To honestly and realistically understand the process of how to accomplish great ends in life is a *sine qua non* of all true advancement.

We go forth in life by virtue of higher inspired vision of that which is yet to be. Failing this— great and mighty wind—we sink back into the depths of moral and spiritual obscurity, back into those states we should have already overcome. But true commitment and perseverance and an uplifted outlook on life, by grace of God on High, can deliver us all from this.

What is it to say that one is a *metaphysician*, except that one thinks thoughts, feels feelings, wills actions, which is to say, exercises and experiences as a spirit: is affected and, in turn, has effect, both by and upon all those who one surround—and this is all of us! Praise God! Amen.

[END NOTEBOOK.]

Recent Inspirations from Labor Day, Sept. 7, 2020. North Shore Lake Tahoe, Nevada, 11 AM-5 PM.

Just west of Thunder Lodge. Smoky but mellow sun shines through. A number of others here.

Honoring Time, Place, One's Body, the Earth: some spontaneous reflections

I celebrate each passing moment of Time. When clear perception prevails in my psyche, I realize that each moment is unique and special and indispensably ties all so-called past with all so-called future. And what's more, this great transcendence we call Time unites us all—all diversely evolved beings—at each special moment in some *indispensable universal happening*. Truly it is so. Praise God! Amen.

Going for swim now along with other nature-honoring people recognizing their place as Earthlings. This thought occurs to me: What does one's Earthly body say most of all other than "Here I am"? Yet, each one of us is much more than just our physical body or even the physical world in which we dwell.

There is a special quality that comes from solitary living. One grows accustomed to one's own company and is not afraid to look at, hear and even know oneself. —Now to some, such who seek the solitary life may seem strange. Yet, is it not from such solitary lives that amazing breakthroughs and marvellous, great treasures have come into this world… from such as these seemingly out-of-touch and unaffected pariahs that so much of all that is truly good and blessed and uplifting into this wondrous and diverse, mysterious and evolving, living world has come?… Now, sometimes, in my solitary wanderings, whilst so many are branding me the miserable solitary, in fact, I have entered into such a wondrous, soul-awakening sense of universal connection, harmony and unity, meaning and purpose, that it astounds me how they who so judge me can ever be so very blind!

Funny how some people can be so intolerant, so judgmental concerning those who appear to be a bit different than themselves. Intolerance, prejudice, negative judgment and the like leads nowhere but to violence and destruction of those true and charitable relations that should—indeed!—must come to prevail in this life and in this world.

As concerns all one sees, hears and in any way senses, awakening one's lofty imagination brings the world alive in ways that cause one to recognize the following: That all the world is a communication from Heaven, a medium for our betterment, and that each given moment and the place and state and company and situation one is in, bears a further indispensable revelation leading unto Salvation. Praise God! Amen.

SCHOOL OF HOME ECONOMICS,
University Of Nevada – Reno

THE INDIAN AMERICAN, THE WHITE AMERICAN,
AND THE NATURAL WORLD
By Craig C. Downer for a graduate course term paper. Feb. 10, 1976

That the life styles of the original American Indians and the migrant Europeans who settled here were quite opposed is quite obvious. There are three major reasons for this difference, which I will list as I) Ethical, 2) Cultural, and 3) Technological. All three, however, stem from a basic difference of attitude, which is greatly linked with past evolution, i.e. traditions and long-standing cultural patterns. The Indian lived with the Natural world and revered its plants, animals, and other components. He sought to live in harmony with the free and diverse Nature. In contrast, the European immigrant was imbued with a Lockean philosophy, reflected in both his culture (his agrarian and industrial way of life) and his religion. This philosophy regarded Nature as something to be converted via labor, into a part, or extension, of himself, rather than to be appreciated and lived with (Pearce, p.68). So, naturally, the Indian was seen as a backward heathen, and it was the white man's superior technology which enabled him to evict the redman from his native land.

I. Ethical

In my opinion, ethical attitudes constitute the most important differences in life styles between the paleface and the redskin. Cultures and their technologies can modify if man has the desire and will. Perhaps now that our Western culture is turning the environment into a sort of stale concentration camp for all of life, man can change both of these, taking a lesson from the traditional Indian way of life which was, simply, Respect for Life (Morey).

The ethical factor can be considered under four categories: 1) religious, 2) social mores, 3) attitude towards the Natural world, and 4) attitudes of whites and Indians to each other. All four are tightly interrelated.

Among the Indians there was a much greater connection between religion and phenomena of Nature: birds, plants, animals, trees, stars, sun, moon, and winds were all incorporated into a naturalistic veneration of the Great Spirit which was believed to underlie all of these (Morey, p.ix; Oswalt, ch. 6). You might say the Church was the whole world for the Indians; and, therefore, they sought to live "in a sacred manner".

In the Buffalo Dance of many of the Plains Indians, medicine men would call the buffalo to give themselves for the nourishment of the tribe, invoking the Great Spirit to direct this (Dary, p.61). At times, this dance would last up to 2 or 3 weeks. A white man who joined a Sioux tribe in Nebraska describes the "deep solemnity and reverence", with which the tribesmen would chant to the Great Spirit, or "Wetouka", asking His blessings before going on their hunt (Belden, pp.34-35). An Ottawa tale of heaven tells of idyllic, natural lands full of all kinds of animal and vegetable life, deer cascading freely, etc. This tale also suggests the idea of a predestined purpose for one's life on Earth (Belden, p. 488).

The religion of the Caddooan-speaking people, horticultural dwellers of the river valleys adjacent to the Eastern prairies, identified underlying supernatural forces of Nature with various animals which seemed to embody them (Holder, p.51). These same people performed their communal bison hunts of the summer growing season with much solemn ceremony, incorporating many religious elements (Holder, p.48). Religious ceremonies were greatly involved with the planting, growing, and harvesting of crops (Holder, pp. 135-36). Religion among the more strictly nomadic tribes, e.g. Apache, Crow, and Arapaho, tended to be more private (Holder, p. 127). In a recent conference on child education, a Crow Indian described his religion as "touching everything with a sacred element". He also explained how, to the traditional Indian, all beliefs were tightly interwoven, making it hard to separate any categories such as religious from social or cultural (Morey, p.9).

Among the Laguna Pueblo Indians of New Mexico, there is the tradition of regular evening religious activities during which all children pray to the Supreme God, directing their adoration toward the moon and stars, and asking for the protection of wildlife as well as their own tribal hunters (Morey, p.133). Here they acknowledge a <u>common good</u> which is shared by both man and other life forms. It was the age-old tradition of many Indians to leave a portion of their prey for the consumption of other flesh-eating birds and animals for good luck and for the sake of the animals themselves. It was believed and taken to heart that there was a purpose for all beings (Morey, p.138) and things regardless of whether it served mankind—an attitude diametrically opposed to that prevailing among many whites, especially those of the early frontier days.

Animals were used as symbols of worship. Many of the Plains Indians so dependent on the buffalo would pay tribute to this burly beast by painting him on their clothing, tipis. etc. As a reminder of the important part the buffalo played in their lives, these symbols helped generate respect for the animal. Again, this attitude is quite opposite to that of the whites. For the Whiteman took for granted the things of Nature, regarding them with indifference and taking from them whatever he could get away with.

The Indian sought to know the connection between all outer phenomena and their inner existence. This connection he called Magic and in his dreams he felt he achieved an intuitive perception of the causative, underlying forces of Nature (Morey, p. 141). The esoteric priests and Indians of a tribe were not worshipping the stars and sun, animals and plants themselves, but the underlying force behind them all (Morey, p.139). To put it simply, Magic was the ability to communicate with the inner being of another plant, animal, man, or even the physical world of rocks, waters, sky, and fire. It involved reading the signs of Nature (Morey, p. 144). God was learned through Nature, not with the brain only, but in conjunction with the heart (Morey, p.140).

In regards to the natural world, religion for the white man was dogmatic, taken verbatim from the Bible according to interpretations that justified the European attitude and life-style. This attitude was one of uncompromising <u>Order</u>. In other words, order would be imposed upon the Natural world strictly according to civilized man's desire. Nature would be made to produce for man, and if it did not, it had no right to exist. The Indians were regarded as indolent, lazy, worthless, and their religion as a convent of witches and wizards holding them in familiarity with Satan (Pearce, p.26). Their lack of the property concept was "uncouth" and their failure to till the land forfeited their rights to it. For Puritans, as for Pilgrims before, land tenure was demonstrated from theology. God's commandment was to occupy the Earth, increase, and multiply. As the Puritan leader, John Winthrop stated: 'the white man has the right to cultivate all uncultivated land, therefore, he has a Divine right to possess Indian lands' (Pearce, pp.20-21; & Fey). Thomas Jefferson wrote in 1784 that "those who labor in the Earth are the chosen people of God, if ever He had a chosen people" (T. Jefferson. 1784. Notes on the State of Virginia). Nature was the Chaos and civilized man: God's instrument to reform this Chaos. The white saw himself as the savior of the Indians (Chamberlin).

II. Cultural

Culturally, the white regarded himself as vastly superior to the Indian. Agriculture was "A" on the list of civilized priorities. The three steps in the march of civilization, i.e. colonialism, were: 1) exploitation of moveable wealth by the labor of the natives, 2) final removal of natives, and 3) ultimate occupation and utilization of the land (Holder, p.139).

Among the whites, a strong Work Ethic prevailed. Wealth was a sign of God's favor and the more laborious a man was, the more virtuous. The Indian, on the other hand, labored to feed, clothe, and shelter himself and his tribe only when necessary. Work was not valued as an end in itself; more highly valued was the enjoyment of life, beauty, and wisdom. The Earth was analogous to the Mother's breasts: plowing was like "tearing them with a knife", according to one Indian's vivid terminology (David, p.85).

The culture of most Indian tribes was a combination of horticulture and hunting-and-gathering. Many tribes along the eastern edge of the Great Plains practiced intensive cultivation of fertile river bottoms. These farmer-hunters included the Mandan, Caddo, Omaha, Osage, Oto, Ponca, Quapan, Witchita, Iowa, Kansas, and Missouri (Josephy, p.254). In all tribes it was the women who did the gardening. The men went on hunting trips once or twice a year, usually to the Plains in search of buffalo. Other than this, they kept themselves prepared for war or made war. "Farther to the West were nomads who lived solely by hunting—Comanche, Kiowa, Arapaho, and Plains Apache" (Josephy, p.254).

Even the most nomadic tribes of the High Plains spent their winters in villages (Eggan). These included those tribes driven West: the Teton Sioux of South Dakota, the Pawnee, the Crow, the Kiowa, the Arikara, and the Cheyenne (Josephy, p.159). They stored fruits, nuts, and other edibles gathered in late summer in hoards near their winter camp (Haines, p.19). They also cached dried meat, including the mixture of dried buffalo meat and berries called "pemmican". The advent of Spring called for the planting of small patches of corn, beans and sunflowers. The two hunts they went on were in the Fall and in the Spring, right after the snow melt. Often the Fall hunt would last 3 months. During this time, their women accompanied them. However, the very young and very old along with a few sturdy women were left to mind the gardens and preserve the village.

The Pawnee, famed horsemen of the Plains, utilized a variety of food sources. In the Spring, acre-sized gardens were prepared for cultivation in which beans and squash were planted. These were planted at the mouths of ravines where soil was fertile. Also, good advantage was taken of wild edibles, of which the wild potato was the most important. Berries, wild plums, cherries, mushrooms, roots, and seeds for vegetable and elk, deer, bear, otter, raccoon, and dog for animal were some of the many wild feed sources touched (Oswalt, p.256-57).

The Indian's was a life that sustained itself from a variety of sources and sought to live with the natural diversity and free ways of Nature. Even the erratic wanderings of the buffalo did not cause the Indian any great consternation; but he adapted his hunting routes to these animals. When the horse became a part of the Indian way of life, the advantage of riding horseback did not change the Indian's basic, semi-nomadic life style (Roe, Wilson).

The white man, on the other hand, projected an unbending agricultural way of life onto the Plains environment. However, the initial open range era of the mid-19th century allowed the cattle to roam more or less freely as the buffalo had (Ryden, Dary). But when the Homestead Act of 1862 opened the Plains and Prairies to parceling, the way was paved for disaster. Farmers accustomed to the more humid regions of the East or of Europe, brought their fences, crops, and animals, little realizing that the Great Plains was the greatest grazing area in the world, perfect for wandering herds (Ryden, p.146). Rivers were far apart and the well-adapted buffalo could go for three or more days between waterings (Dary). As the precipitation was much slighter than in the East, the Plains needed longer recovery time between grazings. Therefore, a nomadic way of life for both buffalo and their hunters was indicated as the healthy way. Farms, however, eventually led to overgrazing. And, also, the overstocking of the ranges by cattlemen (occurring in the latter half of the 19th century) started a process of erosion that, combined with plowing, was to reduce vast areas of this lush vegetation to a virtual wasteland—a phenomenon familiar to much of the civilized or once-civilized world. Six months of uninterrupted grazing could interfere with the necessarily rapid seeding cycle of grasses— this interference the introduction of barbed were upon the Plains in 1873 assured (Ryden, p.145). As many of the homesteads or fenced pastures were too far from water to properly irrigate, wind ripped the fertile topsoil from their plowed fields or overgrazed pastures. The Indians marveled at the inordinately bright sunsets over the Plains, thinking it denoted the wrath of the Great Spirit.

Technically speaking it was caused by the great quantities of dust that were blown up into the sky. They also wondered why the white chose to put cows on the Plains rather than leave the buffalo—which required much less care.

By 1934, twenty-five-million acres of Plains had been plowed and abandoned to erosion. Such land was not even good for grazing. And the range land itself had deteriorated by 67% (Ryden, p.208). It was then that the Taylor Grazing Act (1934) was passed. Still, however, the public lands were given over to the use of the livestock industry, which tended to control the U.S. Grazing Service, later Bureau of Land Management, U.S. Dept. of the Interior almost entirely. By the time of the Dust Bowl, an area about the size of California had been irretrievably converted to a wasteland, fit for nothing but a few hardy weeds, and another area about three times the size of California had been deteriorated to such a state that thousands of years of rest would be required to restore the soil.

This is one effect of the "order" of the white civilization. Where there once was a variety of buffalo, elk, antelope, deer, wild horses, rodents, birds, and a variety of grasses, trees, and shrubs—all thriving in a healthy interrelationship, there now were a few hardy weeds, a few non-native grasses man had introduced, a few crops, and the omnipresent cattle and sheep, both of which certainly deserve to be called the "Scourges of the Earth". But really it is the men who place them in such unnatural situations that deserve this title.

Yet, because of modern-day agriculture, the human population has swelled like a balloon in the U.S. and the world over. Living standards and luxury has likewise risen in most Western countries. But how long can this last?! The Indian may not be so unwise when one considers how long he lived in America without degrading the life community. Though records of his arrival on this continent may be in excess of 40,000 B.P., there is firm record of his inhabitation from 12,000 B.P. (Michener, p. 207). The haughty arrogance of Western man might be somewhat daunted if the record of Time is considered—and also the quality of life, meaning not just luxury for man, but an appreciation and preservation of the natural diversity and freedom of the Earth.

Roe has noted that it seems very hard for our nation to change the Indian's mental attitude (Roe, p.371). His eon-engraved nomadic way of life has remained in spite of superficial appearances—and for a good reason!

III. Technological

It is quite obvious that it was the whiteman's advanced technology which enabled him to overcome the Indians of America. A similar story is found in every colonial acquisition the world over. It should be mentioned, however, that were it not for the invention of the repeater rifle in the 1870s (Dary, p.66) and, perhaps, the Winchester Carbine* .44-calliber, the story of the West might have turned out differently—the fierce, equestrian Indians with their bows and arrows holding their territories

---

* The repeater was used to exterminate the Indians, the Winchester carbine to exterminate the buffalo, which accomplished the destruction of the Indians nomadic life-style—his "wildness".

and way of life instead of relinquishing them (Haines). However much there is to be said on the great contrasting technologies of the Indian and the White, I will dwell on a philosophical aspect of this factor during the rest of this paper.

—Most Americans as indeed, most people in our modern day and age, give the appearance of being subjugated to the workings and dictates of a gigantic Machine of man's own devising. It is no wonder that too many have so lost sight of the precious quality of all life forms that they regard machines as of more intrinsic value than other lives—than living creatures, preferring to live with machines than with a diverse life community. Man has become callous and indifferent to the plants and animals that inhabit this Earth. And those that do not fall into the designs of his technologies, he pays little or no attention to. The tractor has replaced the horse; pavement has replaced grass; and artificial lighting, the sun and moon! Other people are about the only life forms many people seriously consider. But this is a sorry mistake when it is considered how very dependent we are on the photosynthetic plant, the decomposing bacteria, and the grazer. Also, we might very well be destroying not only the Natural world about us, but our proper place in it as well.

I would propose that we utilize our scientific advancements not to make a machine, a factory, or a farm of the world, but rather a harmonious community of all life forms where such a thing as Freedom is again known. I would propose an Ecological Way of Life. Even if we had to work harder for this goal and even do without certain luxuries, the preservation of life's home on Earth—instead of just Man's alone—would be well worth it!

—When Washington Irving made a tour of the Prairies in the early 19th century, he described a beautiful land abounding in all kinds of life: deer and antelope leaping gracefully among the woods and over hill and dale, buffalo thundering impressively over the sward, and wild turkeys squawking in the woods. He described the Osage Indians as "stately fellows, simple in garb and aspect with fine Roman countenances", with a true reverence for all forms of life, leading as free life as he had yet seen (Irving, p. 21). Hs even compared the Prairies with, what was to him, the most idyllic of lands—civilized England. All he thought the Prairie needed to be complete was a few mansions tucked away here and there and some cattle or sheep peacefully grazing (Irving, p.147). His description of the star-strewn night under the Prairie sky is truly breath-taking—or at least to imagine how it was.

Ironically enough, it was Irving's own people from England and other European climes, together with their cows, that came and transformed the free Prairies into a sort of monotonous land of farms and factories, smoke and pollution. Would it be possible to change all this so that men could learn to live with their environment, learning a variety of ways of living with the Natural world, instead of converting Nature into a sort of farm?!

I believe it is possible if man would only wish it and be willing to try. It may be our only hope. And, certainly, the only hope for Earth's remaining the Free home of Life, where evolution can proceed at a variety of levels and for the Purpose of all Life!

Sources

Belden, George P. 1871. Belden, The White Chief, or Twelve Years: Among the Wild Indians of the Plains.

Chamberlin, J.E. 1975. The Harrowing of Eden: White Attitudes Toward Native Americans. Seabury, N.Y.

Dary, David A. 1974. The Buffalo Book. Avon

David, Jay. 1972. The American Indian: The First Victim. Morrow, N.Y.

Eggan, Fred. 1966. The American Indian: Perspectives for the Study of Social Change. Aldine, Chicago.

Fey, Harold E. & D'Arcy McNickle. 1970. Indians and Other Americans: Two Ways of Life Meet. Harper & Row, New York.

Haines, Francis. 1970. The Buffalo. Crowell, N.Y.

Holder, Preston. 1970. The Hoe and the Horse on the Plains: a Study of Cultural Development Among North American Indians. U. Neb., Lincoln.

Irving, Washington. 1956 (1825 orig.). A Tour of Prairies. U. Okla., Nor.

Josephy, Alvin. M. 1961. The American Heritage Book of Indians.

https://www.amazon.com/Heritage-Narrative-Introduction-President-1961-1963/dp/B006SVH4PO

Michener, James A. 1974. Centennial. Fawcett. Ch. IV

Morey, Sylvester M. & Olivia L. Gilliam, Editors. N.D. Respect for Life: Report on Conference at Harpers Ferry, West Virginia on the Traditional Upbringing of American Indian Children.

Oswalt, Wendell H. 1966. The Land Was Theirs: A Study of the North American Indian. Wiley, N.Y.

Pearce, Roy Harvey. 1695. Rev. Ed. The Savages of America: A Study of the Indian and the Idea of Civilization. John Hopkins, Baltimore.

Roe, Frank Gilbert. 1955. The Indian and the Horse. U. Okla., Norman.

Ryden, Hope. 1970. America's Last Wild Horses. Ballantine.

Wilson, Gilbert L. 1924. The Horse and the Dog in Hidatsa Culture. IN Anthropology Papers of
the American Museum of Natural History. Volume XV, Pt. 11.

Recommended Readings & Questions To Be Asked For:
The Indian American, The White American, and The Natural World

Readings

1. David, Jay. 1972. The American Indian: The First Victim. Morrow. E772A3. Pt's II & IV.
2. Haines, Francis. 1970. The Buffalo. Crowell, N.Y. SK297H33. pp. 1-88.
3. Holder, Preston. 1970. The Hoe and The Horse on The Plains: A Study of Cultural Development
    among North American Indians. U. Nebr. E78G73H6. All of the book.
4. Morey, Sylvester M. and Olivia L. Gilliam, editors. Respect For Life: The Traditional Upbringing
    of American Indian Children. Waldorf Press. E98C5R47. Ch's 1, 12, 13, & 16.
5. Pearce, Roy Harvey. 1965. The Savages of America: A Study of the Indian and the Idea of
    Civilization. John Hopkins Press. E93P4. Ch's I, II, IV, & VIII. E93P4. C

Questions

1. Ask any Indian what he thinks of his traditional way of life and what lessons, if any, present
    Western society has to learn from it.
2. Ask any farmer or rancher, or son or daughter thereof, what he/she thinks of man's learning to
    live more with Nature by employing sciences to restore more of the original diversity and freedom
    of the land and to learn how we can live as a harmonious and respectful part of Nature.
3. Ask anybody what they think the ultimate result of technology, or the Industrial Revolution, will
    be on the world and if it would be possible to return to living as a part of a free diverse ecosystem
    by employing certain technologies to this end—and whether they would want to do this.
4. What are some ways of developing a more ecological way of life, including those employing
    scientific means?

"WORLD PEACE AND UNITY"

"WORLD PEACE AND UNITY: SOME ASPIRING EXPRESSIONS"
BY CRAIG C. DOWNER, M.S.

Delivered to the full city auditorium of Tbilisi, the capital of Soviet Georgia. Speech was enthusiastically received, including with a standing ovation and cheers from the audience. Speech was translated.

WILDLIFE ECOLOGIST
ADDRESS: P.O. BOX 456
MINDEN, NEVADA 89423
U.S.A.

FOR: OUR SOVIET ODYSSEY - 1986.
TO BE SHARED WITH FELLOW WORLD CITIZENS: THE SOVIET PEOPLES.

DATE: SEPTEMBER 21, 1986

My name is Craig Downer, and it is my great pleasure to be with you today, to share thoughts and feelings, and to come to know the beautiful lands of the Soviet Socialist Republics. It is especially delightful to meet the charming people here.

I have always felt that differences between people are primarily due to misunderstanding and lack of communication. Each person, as each people and each nation, has its unique history, which history to a large extent fashions its present expression. Yet, do we not all march together with universal measure—united in TIME itself, however narrow our current realization of this unity in time may be?!

In the past few centuries, two great and, in many ways, parallel steps have been taken by the Russian and American peoples, respectively. These were the Bolshevik Revolution that led to the Communist state and the American Revolution that gained the United States' independence from England. Both separated the people from rule by an Aristocracy. The Communist state emphasized human progress through communal endeavor and organization, while the American republic stressed individual rights and liberties as pertains practically to the free enterprise system: progress through competition and enjoying the material and social benefits one has earned through his own intelligence, talents, and labor. The French Revolution is another parallel development.

As I see it, both the American and Russian revolutions stressed the value of the individual and his own contributions to society—and both were man-centered.

I would like to suggest, however, a further step in human evolution, a step that will require a greater unity and discipline among mankind on Earth than our planet has before known. It is the Green, or ecological, revolution to which I refer. This advancement will involve the development of man's collective consciousness concerning Nature's importance and Man's place, or niche, among the life community, meaning the plant, animal, unicellular, and even decomposer organisms which form and condition the material home of life and are all inextricably and essentially bound into the Web of Life.

Let us face it: men have acted selfishly and in brazen disregard toward their fellow creatures! However, until recent times, we have been able to so act with relative impunity. But in the 20th Century, scientific advancements have evolved to enable mankind to squander the Earth's resources at a terrifying and an ever-escalating rate, forcing us all to consider just where all this human self-indulgence is leading! The famed French explorer and naturalist, Jacques Cousteau calls man's rape of the Earth "barbaric"—and I call it unconscionable! For the traits of sensitivity and awareness, intelligence and will, are universal to all of life—and it is only in man's conceit that he disregards or denies these miraculous qualities in the rest of the sentient living world which surrounds him. The next great step in man's evolution will not involve his stepping into outer space, but rather, his learning to live correctly, with appreciation and respect, right here on this very Earth! Along with the late and great humanitarian Albert Schweitzer and those of the Hindu and Amer-Indian faiths, I simply suggest that we all become more Reverent for Life, no matter what the form it takes!

As a prime example, man should not wantonly abandon the world's last remaining Tropical Rainforests to the maws of capitalistic greed and human blindness, or even to so-called "necessity"— as is presently occurring! Instead, among the top priorities of the nations of the Earth should be the preservation of these forests through the creation of an International Park in South America's Amazon Basin, and other such "Islands of Hope". This shall be to preserve the very evolutionary cradles of terrestrial plant and animal life on our planet—life that has emerged majestically over the course of hundreds of millions—even billions—of years. And, as Cousteau would be quick to remind us, we should most definitely not forget that original cradle of life: the Sea. But, all too sadly, even Life's Mother Sea we are forgetting.

Because of lack of ecological understanding and spiritual appreciation of Life, Man blithely and obliviously continues his headlong course of self-indulgence and even expects to graduate to other worlds! Yet, he who is master of the world is not he who dominates it for purposes of material self-aggrandizement alone. Rather, the world's true Master—that "Paragon of Animals"—is the man who both understands and loves Life in all its great diversity and intricate interrelationship, and who, in spirit, recognizes his oneness with all that exists. Such a Master shall know how to live correctly and with regard for our living Earth!

If Mankind is to truly unite and establish Peace on Earth, WE must set aside egotism and sit down to converse openly and keenly about the dilemma in which we find ourselves. Through a give-and-take process, recognizing that the grave problems of pollution and ecosystem unraveling we face can best be solved by a change in attitude on the part of all parties concerned, we can realistically unite for a World Peace With Honor . . . through commitment and good will toward all of life, rather than just toward Russian-kind or American-kind—or even Man-kind alone!

I am talking about a willingness to admit the evils of one's own system and the merits of another's and the ability to see a better way that arises through both a synthesis and a transcending of present systems. We need to strike out in new and untried directions, and even to look back to the so called "primitive" ways in order to find solutions to our dilemma. And then we need the Will to manifest the New Way.

However difficult changes are and whatever "knee-jerk" resistance they may meet, the changes of which I speak are required and they are inevitable. I am speaking of a more considerate Way of Life adopted by Man for the Preservation and the Restoration of a free, diverse, and beautiful Life Home on Earth, where mankind will come to see himself as, not only a brother to the other kinds of life, but as a being expressing angelic concern for their welfare.

…Yes, the changes of which I speak are desired by some and needed by all. They must be made, for the very sake of Life on Earth! The awareness and belief and faith in the values that underlie them shall unite Mankind as never before. For with these values in his heart and in his mind, Man shall see a Greater Whole; and in this shall be his exultation, his life's work, and his sustaining faith. For we shall come to perceive the Divine Plan as never before and recognize our Oneness with all that is! We shall both broaden circles and break barriers, as never before…

FOREVER WILD AND FREE

By Craig C. Downer, Wild Horse Ecologist

P.O. Box 456
Minden, NV 89423
ccdowner@aol.com

Speech for Wild Horse Summit conference, Las Vegas, NV, Oct. 12, 2008, organized by ISPMB. Standing ovation and cheers again received at this general assembly of many conference attendees.

Wild horses and burros on public land remain on the very bottom of the totem pole of priorities of both the Bureau of Land Management and the U.S. Forest Service, the two agencies charged by law with protecting and managing them. Yet these two "national heritage species" whose rights to live free are covered by Public Law 92-195 are supported by many millions of ordinary U.S. citizens as well as people worldwide. The extent of livestock grazing and the permittees involved both in their original Herd Areas and in their reduced Herd Management Areas should be clearly spelled out to the public—but this is not being done.

Livestock, big game, and other overlapping uses within the wild equid Herd Areas and Herd Management Areas should be clearly incorporated into the federal government's National Integrated Land System (NILS) data retrieval program as are most of the other land designations such as wilderness, mining claims, livestock allotments, etc. It is quite probable that this is an intentional cover-up for the unfair and illegal treatment that the wild horses and burros are receiving. Last spring a top BLM official plainly told me that virtually all the wild horse and burro Herd Areas (HA's) and Herd Management Areas (HMA's) were leased to livestock grazers. From a close examination of the original 1971 wild horse and burro Herd Areas in relation to overlapping livestock grazing leases, I estimate that over 95% of these original legal areas are being grazed by livestock. And by examining the administratively reduced wild equid Herd Management Areas still occupied by equid herds (scant in relation to livestock), I estimate that over 98% of these legal areas are being grazed by livestock. The latter is all the more objectionable given the large percentage—36%—by which the original Herd Areas have been reduced in setting up these Herd Management Areas (See Table 1 and accompanying Chart).

Original Herd Areas total 53,444,499 acres of which 42,099,454 acres are BLM and 11,345,045 acres are USFS. But reduced Herd Management Areas total 34,441,150 acres of which 29,082,217 acres are BLM and 5,358,933 are USFS. These figures reveal that BLM has reduced its equid-occupied areas by 7,658,302, or 18%, while the USFS has reduced its equid-occupied areas by 5,986,112 acres, a whopping 53%! And this situation is seen to be even more exacerbating when each Herd Area and Herd Management Area is more closely analyzed to reveal the large-scale displacement of the wild equids that has occurred even within what is on paper still an occupied HA or HMA. Consideration of specific HA's and HMA's throughout the West, such as the Spring Range of southern Nevada (Las Vegas BLM Field Office) and the Cedarville California-based Surprise BLM Field Office covering NW Nevada and NE California reveals that not only livestock but also big game are being given entire preference both within the original HA's and even more flagrantly within the greatly reduced HMA's. Indeed, while forage and water rarely seem to be an issue for the established livestock and big game interests, these same resources are almost always portrayed as being too little for the relatively tiny numbers of our nation's remaining wild horses and burros. My overall analysis reveals an effective displacement of the wild equids from at least 75%, or three fourths, of the public lands—both BLM and USFS—to which they are legally entitled as the "principal" presences to be managed for within these original Herd Areas. These HA's were supposed to be determined by where these equids were found at the passage of Public Law 92-195—and I take this to mean not just the tiny portion of Earth the equids stood on at the exact hour and date of the Act's passage, but rather the home ranges of all the bands in every equid herd that was then occupied on a year-round basis.

As concerns how many livestock permittees utilize legal wild equid areas both on BLM and USFS lands and lacking any precise information from our government agencies on this crucial question, I have calculated a logical estimation for such, based on relative proportions. By taking the total number of livestock permittees on the public lands and proportioning this number relative to the percent of public lands that are original wild horse and burro herd areas and also reduced herd management areas, I have obtained the following:

260,000,000 acres/22,000 grazing permittees = 53,444,499 original H.A. acres/X permittees.

Solving for X, yields, X = 4,522 livestock permittees grazing their livestock on the original 53,444,499 legal Herd Areas (BLM) or Territories (USFS) today. This represents 20.6%, or about 1/5th of the livestock permittees on BLM and USFS lands. However, since the occupied HMA's are much smaller than the original HA's, we must calculate as follows:

260,000,000 acres/22,000 permittees = 34,441,150 HMA acres/Y permittees.

Solving for Y, Y = 2,914 permittees grazing their livestock on the reduced 34,441,150 acres in herd management areas/territories today. This represents only 13%, or about 1/8th of the public lands livestock permittees.

Looking at this situation from another angle, of the 4,522 livestock permittees having to originally share the land they graze—by privilege not right—with wild horses and burros, 1,612, or 36%, now no longer have to share. In other words, our supposed public servants have already eliminated the wild horses and burros from the grazing allotments of 36% of the public lands ranchers in spite of the legal right of the horses and burros to live there. To reiterate: this is all the more disturbing because of how marginalized those remaining wild horses and burros have become even within these reduced Herd Management Areas. This lopsided situation constitutes a shameful betrayal of both the wild horses and burros who have a legal right to live here and of the substantial public interest in them that is represented by millions of U.S. citizens, individual people who count upon their public servants in the BLM and the USFS to uphold the law of the land: to do what the unanimously passed Wild Free Roaming Horse and Burro Act of 1971 actually states.

Concerning both Herd Areas and Herd Management Areas, it would be entirely fair to approach the relatively small number of permittees involved with these with the proposal that they reduce or even eliminate their livestock within the legal wild horses and burro areas. This would enable the establishment of truly long-term viable and stable populations in these areas as is consistent with the original intent of the Act. It would also be fair-minded to offer these persons priority treatment for wild horse/burro public tour franchises and population monitoring or habitat enhancing enterprises that are consistent with the purposes of the Act.

Also worth our serious consideration is the suggestion by the late Nancy Whittaker who worked for the Animal Protection Institute. Her idea was that the government issue conservation permits in lieu of grazing permits in the legal wild-horse/burro herd areas as in other land categories such as wilderness, and that the wild equid-supporting public be permitted to bid on these with the aim of freeing the herd areas of competing livestock, especially where in excess, among other conflictive interests. This seems entirely fair and I suggest her insightful proposal be pursued by regulatory and, if necessary, Congressional means.

The percentage of the U.S. population ranching on Western public lands is a miniscule 0.012%, or around one hundredth of one percent; and the percentage of all U.S. livestock feed, including crops, pastures, and range forage, supplied by BLM and USFS lands is only ca. 2%. And this 2% comes at a great economic and even more enormous ecological cost, a cost estimated as at least one half billion dollars annually. But who can put a price tag on the ecological health of Mother Earth upon which the future of life depends?!

Forage consumption by livestock on BLM land amounted to nearly 7 million – 6,835,458 Animal Unit Months [AUM's] in fiscal year 2005. This contrasted with the mere 381,120 AUM's worth of forage that was consumed by wild horses and burros. The latter consumed only 5.6% of the forage consumed by livestock on BLM lands and only 381,120/7,216,578, or 5.3% of the total consumed by both livestock and wild equids. And this percentage is substantially lower still when forage consumed by big game animals is brought into the calculation. I estimate this would bring the figure down to between one and two percent of the forage available on the public domain, or BLM lands, especially considering the priority treatment given to state fish and game agencies by the federal government.

This disparity is even greater on USFS lands where livestock devours 6.6 million AUM's per year yet wild horses and burros eat a mere 32,592 AUM's annually, or the equivalent of only 2,716 wild horses or burros grazing year round. In other words, on USFS lands, wild equids consume 0.49%, or less than ½ of one percent of what livestock consume on Forest Service lands. Combine this with the earlier revealed fact that the U.S. Forest Service has reduced the originally equid-occupied, legal herd areas by 53% and we see to what an egregious extent the Forest Service is "death on wild horses and burros!". Its negative policy is currently reflected in the Pryor Mountain Wild Horse Refuge in Montana where Custer National Forest officials are refusing to acknowledge that the unique Pryor Mountain Spanish mustangs have a legitimate right to live in an area [their seasonally occupied summer highland meadows that they benefited] they occupied at the passage of the 1971 Act.

Livestock are often allowed to strip the very most nutritious forage, during a few months to a half year often in the spring or early summer, leaving what remains in the way of forage for the wildlife, including the returned native wild horses, to fend on as best they can for the rest of the year. Being much less mobile than wild horses and burros, livestock concentrate their grazing pressures in certain areas, especially in and along species-rich stream, marsh, or lake shore habitats known as riparian (which I have experience monitoring with the BLM). Cattle and sheep have destroyed these riparian habitats on a large scale by overgrazing throughout the West—as throughout the world, especially in arid and semi-arid areas–and thus are responsible for the extinction or near extinction of literally thousands of species of plants and animals. The wild horses, on the other hand, do not linger at watering sites or along riparian areas but disperse their grazing pressure much more broadly in the arid to semi-arid West; and as a consequence they greatly reduce dry parched vegetation. Their post-gastric digestive system is perfectly suited to taking advantage of this drier, usually coarser vegetation, as such does not entail as much metabolic energy involved with the more thorough breakdown of this food when compared with ruminant grazers: cattle, sheep, deer, elk, etc. Their digestion also favors the dispersal of the seeds of many native plant species that are not as degraded in passing through their digestive tracts. These involve species that have in many cases co-evolved for millions of years with horses and even burro-like Asses, developing many mutually beneficial symbioses in the process.

Given the length of time equids have evolved here, it would be blind not to recognize the great importance of the equid element in the North American ecosystem. Yet government personnel persist in maintaining that the wild equids do not warrant native wildlife designation. I suggest they visit one of our national monuments by the name of Hagerman Horse Fossil in Idaho and carefully consider the abundant evidence from paleontological science that establishes the horse family, genus, and even modern-day species, *Equus caballus*, as among the most truly native in North America, for most deeply and anciently rooted and of longest evolutionary duration here. The horse as returned native species and the burro as a species with substantial evolutionary roots in North America are proven facts concerning these two national heritage species, but these facts are rarely if ever acknowledged by BLM and USFS officials charged with their protection, and when so, in a way designed to minimize their relevance.

To me it seems the height of ingratitude that of all the species upon which humans inflict their prejudice and spite, it should be these two who have performed such a world of service for mankind over, not just centuries, but approximately seven millennia! Yet their truer place among unfolding life on Earth was and remains in the wild, and particularly here in North American where the vast majority of their evolutionary past history was experienced over many millions of years and with practically no break right up to the present.

In freedom and in the wild, the true vigor of any race or species is preserved! We owe this freedom on the land that gave them birth to the magnificent horses and wise burros. Given sufficient freedom in space and time, they prove that the equid element restores and enhances the ecosystem here in North America, as elsewhere. But they must be allowed to fill their natural niche in a natural habitat of sufficient size to become a long-term viable, stabilized population. And we have not really given them this chance since the early- to mid-19th Century. Many studies have revealed an increase in native biodiversity in areas where wild equids have been so restored, including in southeastern California's Coyote Canyon Wild Horse Herd Area on BLM land, from which lamentably all of the distinctive, Spanish descended mustangs have recently been removed! Seed dispersal and soil building through added humus (both performed by means of fecal deposition) count among the primary ways in which this enhancement is achieved. And there are many other ways I could describe given the time (rolling swales as water catchments; accessing food and water by hoof action both for themselves and other species both in Summer and in Winter, etc.).

—I am very concerned for the approximate 30,000 mainly wild horses but some burros who have been over-gathered and now languish in government holding areas and for whom euthanasia has recently been proposed by BLM officials as a convenient way of solving the crisis they themselves have created. And I strongly urge that these animals be restored to their empty or nearly empty—but still legal—Herd Areas throughout the West. This is the only honorable course of action, and we owe it to them!

I have performed a calculation of the numbers that could be restored based on the various sizes of the legal Herd Areas. Though just the empty Herd Areas in Nevada alone, or in Wyoming alone, could accommodate the 30,000, I recommend that these equids be used to restore more viable herds throughout all the 10 Western states from which they have been unfairly depleted. However, care should be taken to restore the wild equids to their original Herd Areas wherever possible, or if not possible, to Herd Areas as close by to their natal grounds or with as similar habitat types, climates and other conditions as is again possible. Availability of water, forage, shelter and other habitat requirements, of course, should also be considered – and our public servants must learn to stand up to the wild horses' and burros' enemies in securing such vital resources, including summering and wintering grounds and the corridors there between.

Here is a summary by state of where the wild horses and burros could be released into already emptied Herd Areas or Herd Management Areas that contain too few wild equids and whose numbers should be bolstered for greater viability. (See Table 2 & chart.)

In Arizona, 540 wild burros, 35 wild horses proportionally among 8 herd areas according to area size, AML, species designation and habitat factors such as water and forage.

In California, 303 wild burros into 2 herd areas and 2005 wild horses into 13 herd areas.

In Colorado, 659 wild horses into 7 herd areas/herd management areas.

In Idaho, 81 wild horses into 4 herd areas/herd management areas.

In Montana, 294 wild horses into 6 herd areas.

In Nevada, 5,200+ wild horses into 31 herd areas/herd management areas.

In New Mexico 166 wild horses into 3 herd areas/herd management areas.

In Oregon 2,240 wild horses and 10 wild burros into 28 herd areas/herd management areas.

In Utah, 1,085 wild horses and 17 wild burros into 18 herd areas/herd management areas.

In Wyoming, 7,425 wild horses into 29 herd areas/herd management areas, 22 of which are zeroed out and 7 below AML.

Totals: **19,19**0 wild horses and **870** wild burros for total **20,060** wh/b's in **149** ha/hma's.

The additional approximately 10,000 government-held wild equids could easily be accommodated by assigning just AML's to the zeroed-out herd areas. These would be proportional to the size of such as well as water and other resource availability therein. Also, by increasing already assigned AML's that are ludicrously low and disproportionate to the size and resource availability of the original HA's in question many of the excessively gathered wild equids could be accommodated.

Table 2 shows the additional equid numbers that could be, thus, easily accommodated and Table 1 shows other revealing data such as the acreage and percentages of reduction of original herd areas occurring in each state, i.e. elimination of wild equids there from. These estimated additional numbers by state are:

Arizona (15% reduction): 1,000 wild burros/horses;
California (65% reduction): 5,000 wild horses/burros;
Colorado (45% reduction): 1,000 wild horses;
Idaho (12% reduction): 1,000 wild horses;
Montana (83% reduction): 1,000 wild horses;
Nevada (23% reduction): 4,310 wild horses/burros;
New Mexico (77% reduction): 334 wild horses;
Oregon (32% reduction): 1,750 wild horses/burros;
Utah (28% reduction): 1,085 wild horses;
Wyoming (53% reduction): 2,575 wild horses.
Total: 19,054 wild equids

As is readily observed, the federal agencies in most states have already grossly infringed on the wild horses'/burros' legal rights to land and are now proceeding with mop up operations! The additional numbers that should be released into the 10 Western federal wild horse and burro containing states sum to 19,054 wild equids, chiefly horses with some burros.

Summing to the earlier figure, **a total of 39,114 wild equids should and easily could be reinstated into their rightful legal herd areas on federal lands throughout the West administered by the BLM.** This is over 8,000 more than the ca. 30,000 wild equids currently being held. And this evaluation does not take a hard look at the original USFS wild equid herd areas, many but not all of which have been given over to the BLM for management. Since, as earlier indicated, the USFS has reduced its original legal wild equid herd areas by 5,986,112 acres, or 53%, we should well appreciate that it could easily restore many wild equids to these empty by still legal areas throughout the West provided the political will to do so.

To appreciate the extent of unfairness toward America's last wild horses and burros on the public lands where they have legal right – a long tradition that includes other scapegoats such as the buffalo and the Indian himself – I again call your attention to **Table 1 & Chart**. As earlier indicated, the national reduction from the original herd area acreage is 36% and four states have eliminated wild equids from over 50% of their original herd areas: California, Montana, New Mexico and Wyoming. To better appreciate the inequities involved toward the wild equids, we should look at the numbers of acres per individual wild horse or burro both in relation to current existing wild populations and in relation to the planned Appropriate Management Levels (AML's) that our public servants have unjustly established throughout their over 300 legal areas. **Our no-longer-trusted "public servants" – and please take note! – have allowed for only one currently surviving wild horse or burro in the wild per 1,871 acres [ca. 3 square miles] of original legal Herd Areas established by the 1971 Wild Horse Act to protect and preserve them and their freedom,** and well as to manage their numbers in a minimally invasive manner! **And in the greatly reduced Herd Management Areas, there are currently—and again pay close attention!—only 1,206 acres [ca. 2 square miles] per surviving wild equid!** To better imagine the gross unfairness, one entire football field is closely equal to just one acre. These figures come from published BLM data of the current year, 2008. Yet since this evaluation, BLM has been reducing the herds even further than originally planned, depriving several thousand more wild horses and burros of their natural freedom in order to establish the cripplingly low, non-viable **Appropriate Management Levels that would leave 1,253 acres, or football fields, of HMA's per individual wild horse and burro!** —This is a lot of space for the horses to play football and a mockery of the law by any estimate! Also, this is like leaving one wild equid for every livestock permittee.

—BLM planned on leaving only 27,492 wild horses and burros nationwide as of the spring of 2008, though their current total was only 28,563 of which 2,874 were burros and 25,689 were wild horses. This is about the population level of pronghorn antelope that survived in the early part of the last, i.e. 20th, century after the wholesale carnage and plunder of the West by European settlers. This low population level, i.e. 26,000, was just cause for declaring the pronghorn to be endangered and warranting immediate action by authorities to save it. Obviously our two national heritage species are not so valued, since they are being set up for just such a low level. Again, "managing for extinction" comes to mind, both for the wild horses and ten times more for the wild burros!

As a wildlife ecologist who appreciates the wild horses and burros and their freedom, I envision self-contained wild horse/burro reserves both in and around the originally established Herd Areas, including where possible other appropriate areas on both private and public lands. Through ecologically knowledgeable ***reserve design*** that takes into account as many of the short and long term needs of the wild equids as possible, drastic roundups could be avoided, or at least greatly minimized. This can and will be accomplished by incorporating natural boundaries that limit the equids' movements and, only where necessary, by the construction of artificial, semi-permeable equid barriers that allow other species of wildlife to pass through unharmed. Crucial to this plan is that each reserve contain appropriate habitat of sufficient size to support a long-term viable wild horse or burro population of around 1,000 interbreeding individuals. Within each such natural sanctuary, the wild equids will be respectfully treated as the "principal" presence, not relegated to mere token numbers and deprived of basic resources to accommodate a monopoly of livestock and/or big game —currently the case! In these equid reserves, natural checks and balances will be allowed to operate, including natural predators of equids such as the puma and the wolf. With relative rapidity, the herds will attain population stability as part of a special, harmonious give-and-take relationship with each unique occupied ecosystem. And the cruel and ecologically disruptive roundups that have tragically set back the site-specific adaptiveness of the West's magnificent wild horse and burro populations will become a thing of the past! —Thank God!

Every truth- and justice-loving person should ask him/her self: "Is the kind of treatment wild horses and burros are currently receiving fair?! Do not our fellow Earthlings in equine form—who have done so much for us humans—deserve a much better place and consideration in this our shared world?!

We know what interests are displacing these National Heritage Species within the relatively minor portion of public lands to which they have legal right. But it has proven very difficult for wild horse and burro advocates to obtain exact figures on the allocation of resources to livestock and big game within the legal wild horse and burro Herd Areas and Herd Management Areas. I believe these figures are being intentionally hidden from the public precisely because they would reveal such an enormous subversion of the Wild Horse and Burro Act and in order to achieve an even more blanketing public lands monopoly by livestock and big game. among other, interests. **We can rest our case, however, on the fact that our supposed public servants are planning to leave only one wild horse or burro for nearly 2,000 football fields of their original legal herd areas!** This is, indeed a "managing for extinction" at its worse and one with a farcical justification. This intolerable situation boils down to sheer greed and selfishness on the part of some people who have not learned the how and why of sharing, of appreciating another kind, and the greater world we share with all fellow species. (I refer you to the excellent work Las Vegan Cindy Macdonald has done to reveal to the public the gross inequities that are involved in the federal wild horse and burro program [see www.americanherds.com].)

Though the horse is a quickly reverting, returned native wildlife species in North America, complementing many native plants and animals, and though he greatly reduces flammable vegetation, thus preventing catastrophic fires of mounting "global warming" concern today, he is still perversely treated as a destructive exotic by federal officials. This is in conformance with a mainly negative policy toward both the wild horse and burro. The burro species is a member of the ass branch of the horse family, Equidae, which branch had its origin and long-standing evolutionary development in North America. It refills an empty niche that was occupied by very similar Asses in the drier areas of the West and not that long ago, geologically speaking. Both species successfully disperse the seeds of native plants and help build water-retentive and nutritive soils through their feces. Upon these wild equids so much of the native Western ecosystem depends. **And in such, given sufficient time and space and freedom, all individuals and species—including wild horses and burros—ever work in marvelous conjunction!**

"With nostrils flared and mane flying, the horse is an image of beauty and grace with an undying spirit! Although briefly domesticated by man, its awe-inspiring, multi-million-year history and destiny remains in the vast, wide-open spaces of the natural biodiverse and inter-balanced world. And whether corralled or at liberty, its heart remains its own, forever wild and free!"

-Bergamot Brass Works, Inc. 1983

Challenge For Nevada Poetry Society

A Hanukkah Tribute at Christmas

For Nevada Poetry Society Christmas party meeting on Saturday, 18 December 2021.

Being "part Jewish" according to *Ancestry*
And, also once part of a Jewish family
As well as Kibbutz Dan, however briefly,
Though of Methodist Christian upbringing
And still a believer in Christ Jesus
As the *Messiah*, Anointed One,
I thought it befitting
This year 2021
At *Holy Days'* time
To celebrate my Jewish connection, relation—
Or whatever this should be called…
For truly I believe
That we are all related…
For what's the "pure race" anyway?!
And just remember that Jesus Christ
And the original Christians –
Those who truly "walked the talk"

Were Jewish too!
For in ultimate analysis
We are all
Related somewhere, somehow…
One Interconnected Family.
—So, "on with the poem" I say:

Hanukkah, or "The Festival of Lights,"
As it is called,
Is a Remembering and Celebrating
Of the *Menorah* candles
That miraculously burned
Beyond their expected time,

According to the oil supply
That would have lasted only
One day—yet on they burned for eight!

This astonishing event marked
The recovery of *Jerusalem the Golden!*—
And the *Dedication—Hanukkah's* meaning—
Of the Second Temple—
Such a Heavenly Place of Splendor!…
Now, for your information, all this happened
When the *Maccabeans* revolted against
The *Seleucid Empire*—a Hellenized Syria—
During the Second Century Before Christ—
Really not all that long ago…
Then There Was So Much Joy
As I do recall…
A reassertion of *our*
True Hebrew identity,
A throwing off of
What seemed to us a smothering darkness,
One not just physical but spiritual,
For Forth a Pure and Bright Light Shone,
Came to prevail,
A Higher Living Light
That burned—and burneth still!—
Against seemingly insurmountable
Odds according to life's merely worldly view,
Just as that holy miracle of *The True Life who*
Within each and every one
Of our "candle bodies" dwells,
But whose true Godly spirit
Never extinquisheth.
Praise God! I say, Praise God!
And *Hallelujah!* shout!

AN ODE TO BIRDS, BOTH HERE AND GONE

For "Creature Poem" Challenge by Carolyn Dondero. To be read before compassionate Nevada
Poetry Society, Sat. June 18, 2022.

Birds are such beautiful beings when they sing!
They are so musical in the dawn when their voices ring!
Proceeding from them, a special communication I do hear—
some new dispensation from On Far!
To fail to heed their call
would seem a crime unbearable!

Yet, how many of our wonderful birds today
have or are disappearing from the Earth!
How many entire species have gone the way
of the *Dodo*, an unusual species no longer with us here,
having been wantonly massacred on some island
by sailors who didn't give a damn!
No sensitivity had they,
but only followed their base cravings,
butchering all in their destructive path!
They were like so many still are
in this 21st Century that neither most birds
nor most other kinds,
according to science, will survive!
And all this because of our own species—kind?! [double-entendre]

And, so, I uplift my voice in song
unto the High Heaven above.
I do this as an Ode to those Heaven-bound birds
who are no longer present in body here,
or may not be for much longer,
but whom God and Heaven has or shall
most surely welcome!
—In a flash I "see"
All these bird souls, whatever their species,
looking down and with pity upon

this once so alive and beautiful but now dying Earth…
upon all those unfortunate ones
who still manage to dwell here.
This was once a Heavenly place, you know,
but, because of an insane human self-centeredness
and unlimited growth, seems now
to have met its demise in
the human species' insane, unlimited Greed!

Yet, I sure hope and pray not, for perhaps
the many bird spirits *up there* will
sing us some great inspiring
song of redirection and good cheer…
one that will elevate our hearts and minds and wills—
pick us up from out the rut in which we've fallen!
This supreme and avian ode will us redeem…
as each man/woman shall regain
his/her true Moral Compass.
Then we'll pick ourselves up and be on—
to live life with a genuine
Reverence for All of Life, not just those in human form!

In this new and Golden Age we will display
an exalted regard for all interconnected
beings, regardless seeming outward
differences in manifest form or demeanor.
For our shared Purpose and Source lies beyond
all the gross and twisted misconceptions
of an onerous, grubbing mediocrity —
consequence of an abjectly Fallen State!

Instead, we will look forward to
All Life's Onward, Unfolding Future Story
that shall reveal only what's truly Great!
—And our very ability to look forward to this
throughout all ever interconnected
Past, Present and Future times—
why All Life's very Fountain of Youth this is!

DIAGNOSIS AND PRAYER FOR A DYING PLANETARY LIFE COMMUNITY

For reading before Earth-conscientious Nevada Poetry Society on Saturday, May 21, 2022. In fulfillment of Nature/Ecological Crisis Challenge posed by Craig himself.

In the present day and age
those of us who live on Earth are faced
with the most enormous predicament!
Much of this concerns our species'
unwillingness to acknowledge
the utter insanity of unlimited growth,
and expansion, particularly of our population
and its consumption of all this planet has to give.
Basically, this has to do
with our self-vaunting egos and
our limited horizons, particularly as these ignore
the Great Beyond, including the Higher Spiritual Dimension!

Our problem concerns our infatuation with power and control,
and our failure to censor our very own worldly-hemmed-in selves
and ways of living on this Earth, whose intrinsic value we seem to ignore,
as we do our interrelationships with the Greater Family of Life—
all the other species—each valuable in its own right
and as concerns its relation to the Greater Whole.
These all make life possible for and are related to us in human form,
yet how few people today seem to respect this so poignant truth!
Most today seem to place
themselves upon a smug pedestal
of Human Supremacy over all,
and oft use a type
of twisted religion or of science
to justify this—for shame!
They overlook the importance
of most other species, other kinds,
and each one's unique and indispensable
function within the life community as a whole…
however narrowly or broadly defined—
and that must be realized in freedom!

Such arrogance and narcissism then
has led to the shameless plunder
and manipulation of nearly every
fellow species upon this Earth,
as well as their amazingly
distinctive yet interdependent ecosystems,
most of which are sadly dying—
take the coral reefs,
including Great Barrier,
as but one of many striking examples today.
And, just remember:
we humans depend
for our Earthly existence
upon them all.

Most lamentably,
It's many human's devil-may-care
attitude that's bringing about the
end of All Precious Life on Earth
today… or so it seems.

So, for this very reason,
before the breaking dawn
of this new and special day,
I must simply pray…
send up to God in Heaven
and all its over-governing Angels
a most sincere and fervent request—
not just for my own
or even just humanity's
further advantage,
but rather for *the true success*
of All Precious Life Together…
and a request for
True Enlightenment spread out equally
among all my fellows
as concerns that
Magnificent Rest of Life

and humanity's special obligation thereto
and our realization that
we are not apart from
this Greater-Leading-to-Very-Greatest Whole!

For unless such enlightenment occurs,
within the inmost hearts and minds and wills
of us people today—myself included—
and we learn a new and better,
more respectful way of living with
and relating to all the so-called "other"
species who share this world as home
and place of unfolding evolution,
as well as a truer appreciation
of both how and why any ecosystem
actually functions and has come to function
as the outcome of millions of years of evolution,
or unfolding, then I see only our continued
dire destruction of all this most precious
Life on Earth.

This Marvel mustn't be destroyed
due to the blind and monstrous
self-centeredness of Man!
So, help us, dear God, to overcome
our own worst enemy:
That false self who would claim
our conscious identity—
or, rather, this erase—
resulting in a perverse nature,
lacking in Life's true comprehension and
true Charity, true Love!
For this I now and continually do pray,
uplifting my consciousness
unto the Eternal—unto Thou
Who dwelleth upon High!

BEAUTIFUL COMMUNION IN A DREAM

For delivery before august assemblage of the Nevada Poetry Society on 3/19/2022, in Reno.

Sometimes I think there is a greater reality to our life and lives of Dreaming
Than there is in all this awake, worldly life and all its infernal scheming!
Take, for example, the exquisite dream I just had this morning before my awakening:
Such a pure, sweet, and innocent communing!
I sensed a very special branch of Heaven was assuming
Me into some higher dimension
Where a beautiful young lady was present.
She glowed with an innocent radiance that was entrancing!
Then we shared a kiss and this bequeathed a measure
Of such pure joy and pleasure
That this lone and apparently aging bachelor
Felt himself rejuvenated—quickened and infused
With such a wonderful sense of coming alive again…
Fulfilled in some amazing and unexpected way,
Brought back in touch with all that truly matters—
An essential part of his true reason for living, for being here—
Felt himself truly blessed!
And, so, I ask you: "Who could ask for more?"
And if you dismiss this vivid dream as unreal,
I have only this to say: it was truly real
Though on some higher—yet ever interrelated—
Plane of consciousness.
The vivid experience of this dream
I shall long remember, treasure!
And, yet, I ask: Just who was this beautiful young lady
With whom I shared—however fleetingly—
Such a precious moment's exquisite joy?
Somehow, I just inwardly know:
She fits within some Beautiful
And Universal Scheme…
One unfolding joyously throughout all times—All Time!
She must have in this appointed dream

By some higher spiritual means
Fulfilled some basic necessity
For which I had unknowingly screamed.
Could this be proof of some Higher Ordering…
Some ongoing perfecting evinced magnificently
Within a Love-Bound Dream?
Most sincerely I do believe so; and so
Give thanks unto The Supreme Being—Our Universal God!

Impressions After Returning from A Trip To Las Vegas and Southern Nevada
(This is an example of rhyming couplets with alliteration on the first syllable of words.)
October 15, 2022 challenge for Nevada Poetry Society

Vehicles, engines growling, gears grinding, groaning!
Multitudes of people manacled to machines—Life's moaning
Upon bearing so many burly abuses!
Seemingly mindlessly oblivious people pursuing mundane uses,
Caught up in the moment, fraught by forgetfulness of Time,
Forgetting the past, neglecting that there is—Alas!—sublime
Future and an indispensable Juncture in the here and now
Between all that has gone before and that Tao
Which takes us to what yet lies in store and makes us still more
Perfect than before realized—that we can more truly adore!

LIFE'S TRUE THRILL! (a *Minute* poem)

Composed Sunday 3/16/2022

By contemplating noble Truth's
regaining, youth's
made possible—
and conscience full!
For then potentialities
spring up with ease…
that long ignored
is now adored!
Obeying God who's known within,
we vanquish sin…
confusion kill…
know Life's True Thrill!

My Visitation by a Pair of Mountain Tapirs—a True Vision

Poem conceived while remembering my dream on Saturday 7/22/2023.

On May 11th, 2023, right about dawn,
I had a wonderful dream,
Or, better yet, a splendid vision—
Truly a joyous occasion!
For like two angels there appeared to me—
Two beautiful Mountain, or Andean, Tapirs—
—So splendidly!

Now adeptly fastened were they
Upon a steep, cloud-forested slope,
They stood in a place
where I had tracked them
Relentlessly for years.
The plants, the birds, the bees, *et cetera*,
Seemed all so familiar, yet enhanced,
Like some special Andean branch
Of Heaven laden with delicate orchids
And festooned with jewel-like hummingbirds
Darting so deftly around.
—Aye! 't was a bright mid-morning
Full of a unique—glorious sunshine!

For years in my field studies,
I was used to have them scamper off
Whenever—binocular and radio-tracker in
hand— I would draw nigh.
But this *vision time* was different.
For now they sought me out,
Did me espy—overjoyed
To hear and see—
In many ways perceive me.
And I more fully sensed and perceived them
Within some higher, vitalized dimension.

Adult tapir on the slopes of the Sangay Volcano
in Sangay National Park –© Craig C. Downer

So robust and alive were they—
Then a remarkable happening:
Like a celestial duet
Standing side-by-side,
In a flash, they extended
Their prehensile proboscises in tandem.
Amazingly, these versatile organs became,
Elongated, coppery-colored, burnished flutes
Then all of a sudden they sonorously sounded out
A most mesmerizing, mellifluous, heartfelt rendition
Of Beethoven's Wonderful *Ode to Joy!*
Miraculously, this communicated
Their pure and special love.
That powerfully enveloped me!
—A supreme gift was this!
Verily uplifting me
To Heaven's Tapir Branch.

In this special Heaven I was welcome—
An honored member and given a surprise.
For after the joyous Beethoven song
They performed a second wonderful tune
And with vigorous, montane flare!
Astounded was I that
This exquisite creation summed up
Long eons of living in the Andes here—*aqui!*.
This happening consciously
United me with them—
Showed me that *In Spirit*
We are all One…
However mysteriously we come
To realize this most remarkable fact of life.

Upon retrospect I felt
This wonderful gift
Had something to do
With all those many
Long, laboriously striving years

During which my Andean companions and I
Had worked both to understand
And to *Save* these great
Endangered wonders
In their fantastic Andean home
And to save their natural home as well:
In fact a Globally life-preserving one—
And headwaters of Mighty Amazon!

These woolly tapirs'
Natural palaces are composed
Of cloud forests and *paramos*,
A type of moorland above the trees.
They extend clear up to *Volcan Sangay's*
Snowy, glistening white glaciers.
My trusty Andean companions and I
Bravely summitted 17,300-foot Sangay
On December 6th, 1991 *Ano Domini.*
Crown jewel of *Parque Nacional
Sangay* is this volcano,
Helping make it a *World Heritage Site.*

…Before I close, I have this to say:
From the two tapirs of my vision,
Arose two most vivid melodies.
And just the thought of these
Is enough to uplift me at any time.
Their very transcendent existence
Carries me up and away
Unto their own
Special branch of Heaven.

…The upshot of this precious vision
Is their Special Love and this Love's Power.
It inflamed my own heart too;
And I believe it can transform
The whole, wide world
Both for this precious
Tapir pair's own sake

And for all their Sangay family,
As well as for all their kind.
…And like unto this blessed vision
To me right now
There seems no greater one.
Praise God! I say, Praise God! Amen!

Two Free Verse Poems for Nevada Poetry Society Challenge for April 15, 2023.

OVERVIEW
Composed 4/8/2023)

You know,
Oh! my soul!
That I just love it when
You go in
To *Overview* state,
As with your High Dreams—
Sometimes spanning many lifetimes!—
And then
Are moved to so eloquently,
Idiosyncratically,
Express these
Inspired panoramas.

For they reveal
All Life's greater,
Higher meaning,
Purpose, aim!
For in them dawns
Greater Truth-revealing Light—
showing forth the Way!—
Tying together
All Past, Present, and Future,
And leading so perfectly
Unto Salvation!
Praise God! Amen.

MANY MIRRORS

Conceived 4/5/2023, mid-morn.

Sometimes
I feel very snug
When I'm alone…
So-called "alone"…
For is one really ever?
At other times
A sense of desperation—
Even horror sets in!
Then I simply
Breathe deeply,
Recenter,
Take stock
In what
I've ever realized
And *still am*…
To know
That all I experience,
Whether *external* things
And processes
Or fellow *internal* beings—
And this *one right here!*—
Are ever further clarifying
Mirrors unto both my and our greater,
Truer, and more perfect *Self*.
– Praise God! and Hallelujah! shout.

Poem about Facing the Obvious

Composed 8/6/2023, in honor of my dear sister Catharine on her birthday.

In life we should not
Overlook the obvious.
This particularly concerns our challenges…
The so-called "problems".
Let's see these rather
As stepping stones…
Invitations to higher planes
Of self-realization and perfecting…
And inter-relationally as well…
Concerning the collective and the Common Good.
Now, the reason we sometimes overlook—
What most needs critical examination—
Involves our moral laziness,
Self-complacency and backsliding.
One may think
He/she can get away with this,
But such smug irresponsibility
Only digs us into a deeper hole.
And, so, I urge us all
To honestly come clean—
To atone and come to grips
With all manner of blindnesses
Concerning what's of greater importance
Than petty-minded habits and attachments
That get an unearned pass,
Disregard Life's Greater Truth
And would be our undoing
Save for our ability to face up!
Being an Ecologist,
A conscientious examiner of all life's interrelations,
I can tell you with some considerable urgency
That we humans need to rectify
Our relationships not just to others in human form
But to all the Great Rest of Life!

Furthermore, as concerns this most crucial challenge today,
Please just do not forget to pray
That your actions and lifestyles
Will take on a true Virtue…
A Heavenly Grace that will
Save the day!

Strangely Joyful Encounter

Conceived 8/29/2023.

You know, oh my soul,
Hardly any experience's
More faith-restoring,
Rejuvenating and joyful
Than when seemingly
By chance we meet again
Though apparently
We have not met before
During our present lifetime,
For a strong recognition
Instinctively between us happens…
As shared experiences and goals—
A wealth of associations springs up!
Some special relationship
Is conjured by the Imagination.
But just what's imagination? I ask now
How can so many conceptions,
Thoughts and their ever-linked feelings
Be so instantly revived?
—Such seems a great wonder, indeed!
Must this not proffer
Some greater fulfillment
Destiny has in store?
An important Thread
Back into our unfolding

Lives has woven itself,
However short- or long-ago.
They've taken up the weave, re-knit again
Within Holy Time's August Dimension…
This Flow that works
Upon the Universal Scale.
I remark its great immensity
But am not intimidated thereby,
For this strangely meant reunion
With a fellow soul,
Proves to me
Just how well-related we all are,
As all our lives parallelly unfold,
Betimes seemingly separate,
Yet, ever really together
Within that awesomely restoring
Continuum of God's!

SWEET BIRD OF LOVE—an *Arkaham* Ballad

For April 2021 *Arkaham* poetry challenge of Nevada Poetry Society.

There is a subtlety to love
  It's fine and pure and gay…
Awakening all that's so good
  Restoring health just like it's food…
Intense as Sun midday!
  Experience of love that's true
Comes not at mere command
  But like refreshing dew of morn
This sparkling blessing in us's born
  —Like bird that's out of hand! Fly
on, sweet bird, unto the Light!
  May no one cut your wings
Nor heart's desire for All that's pure.

Your destiny for this is sure!
For this you'll ever sing!

The Art of Words and What It Reveals

(Conceived 5/27/2023 for Nevada Poetry Society June challenge about the art of poetry.)

Words are such amazing things!
They are a being's unique creations,
Yet ever unfold in relation to all fellow co-strivers!
They display the very derivation of all outward phenomena —
That powerful principal of ongoing, unfolding,
Universal and all-uniting Life—
Ever imbued in all its multiple manifestations
With that Ever-Higher Meaning
That transcends all mere outward things…
Including words that have been made manifest.
For Meaning is of Godly essence—
Spells out and leads to very Salvation:
Very universal, all-connecting Beingness
Taken in all its glorious wholeness and perfection:
That from which all mere objects, times,
Words, notes, songs, stories, lives—
You name it!—most fascinating spring!

THE BIRDS SO BLITHE!

Conceived Jan 27 & Feb. 6, early mornings & typed mid-morning of Feb. 6, 2022. This is the *Rondeau* form for February 19th Nevada Poetry Society challenge.

The birds so blithe!—they chirp away,
Communicate each in its way.
Just like people they talk and sing.
Throughout the world their voices ring!
And certain is: they can make hay!

Their energy is oh so fay!
They hop around as if to say:
I am the Queen! I am the King!
The birds so blithe!

So let them live and love and play
Now and forever and a day.
With purpose they with zip and zing
Fulfill their roles and do take wing
When Called by God the Course to Lay!
The birds so blithe!

Native Andeans –Craig C. Downer

THE TINKLING-BELLED CARAVAN

For *Cameo* challenge. Inspired by a dream with a feel of prophecy during night of March 18, 2022, ca. 2:30 AM. Worked up on March 20th. Refined April 5, 2022. For Nevada Poetry Society meeting of April 16, 2022.

I.
I had
remarkable dream
perceived some strangely familiar
bright people
in a strong, horse-drawn caravan,
heard clear tinkling, bright sleigh bells
—Music!

II.
Then a
wonderful inner
voice informed me this caravan
had been with
me before but in another time,
even as I perceived it now
—Constant!

III.
Somehow
I knew that it would
be with me again in future,
that over
time, oft separated by long
periods, its gentle bells
—Greet me!

IV.
And then
surged an inner voice
saying special soul-reviving
beauty's in
the very eeriness with which
mystic caravan returns
—Welcomes!

Nature Poem: Craig's Challenge to Fellow Nevada Poetry Society poets for May 21st, 2022 plus Invitation to special wild horse rally on April 23rd in Carson City

In the urgent and timely spirit of Earth Day, my challenge to the Nevada Poetry Society is to compose a poem that deals with the current crisis in our world, our precious living Earth, or Gaia. I want you to ponder deeply the full significance of the marvelous life community, or ecosystem, and all its many diverse kinds: plants, animals, fungi; photosynthesizing plants, consumers, recyclers; from the macro to the micro in scale; from the waters, earth and air; from below and above Earth's surface—or on it—where-ever, whatever, and how all this relates overall to make life possible—our great interrelated Family of the Living and the Transcended also. Think, if you like, about the giant Redwood trees that grow near us, but are now under serious jeopardy for their survival due to Global Warming, or choose the giant Sperm Whales or other type sea creatures that likewise struggle to survive. (I recommend here some of the passages from Samuel Taylor Coleridge's "The Rime of the Ancient Mariner" that deeply contemplated humans' relationship to all the Great Rest of Life, the wondrous fishes of the sea, the mystic and phenomenal Albatrosses, etc. Or chose the tiniest but multitudinous bacteria, algae or even viruses and how all these interrelate and make life possible for all of us here when allowed to freely fulfill their indispensable roles and balance out Life's Great Whole. —I challenge you to really "step up to the plate" here, because the Earth's ecological crisis today cannot, with good conscience, be any longer ignored or pass un-responded to! Each one of us is responsible! So, feel free to use any poetic form or length in grappling with this most urgent challenge for all humans living on Earth today—for Gaia's sake!

Also. I take this opportunity to invite you to come next Saturday, April 23rd, 2022, between 1 pm and 4 pm to the **Wild Horse Freedom Rally** in front of the Nevada State Legislature building and just south of the Nevada Capitol at 401 South Carson Street, Carson City, Nevada 89701. I will be speaking for both the wild horses and the wild burros and there will be musicians and several other speakers. A professional actress, horse-lady and wild horse advocate Fia Perera with be MC'ing the event. More information on this event (planned for every State Capitol) can be found at www.wildhorsefreedomrally.com and at my website https://thewildhorseconspiracy.org. Concerning this event see The Action Hour program with Lindsey Baker. I was on this concerning the wild horse and burro crisis and what can be done to restore the legal herds and their legal habitats to viable levels and in natural freedom as the principal presences in their legal areas—as the Wild Free-roaming Horses and Burros Act intends. The link here is: https://fb.watch/c9JUQS_Pdc/

THE VAST AND OPEN SEA, a *Sicilian tercet*.

For May 20, 2023, Nevada Poetry Society meeting. Challenge by Patsy Gehr of Tucson, Arizona.

The vast and open sea
Of personal experience
Is real as life can be!

In this, we're all participants—
Each valid, special, true,
And bound to make great difference!

All in Great Fullness: Time.
So when you're called to play your role,
Clear mind, tune in to Spirit Divine!

Image Sunset Sunday: At Lands End in San Francisco,
from whiskeytangoglobetrot website

THREE DIVERSE LIMERICKS AT CHRISTMAS TIME
(What is their relation?)

Composed 11/20/22. For 12/17/22, Christmas party of Nevada Poetry Society at Wynn's.

Let's all go to the place: Limerick! It
has rich history, but the trick You
must learn: Not the butt
of its rhyme—this is what
you must do to not fall on its slick!

Christmas Time—'tis a fine time of year!
It's a time we can all be so dear
to those near and the other,
to one's sister and brother!
'Tis a time so splendid—let's be clear!

Mirth seems good for a while but do not
be beguiled by false lures that are hot
as the hell that does lurk
behind veils that do irk
when unmasked they seem not so hotshot!

TIME PASSES, AUGURS WELL—A *RONDINO* (slightly modified rhyming pattern)

Composed 8/21/2021. For Nevada Poetry Society's October 2021 *Rondino* challenge.

TIME DOES TRANSCEND,
PASSES ALL TEMPORARY MOMENTS, STATES, CONDITIONS,
AUGURS EVER TO LIFE'S VERY GREATEST END!
—WELL ONE **NOT** ITS SUPREME MEANING SHUN!
PASSING FROM "HERE TO ETERNITY"
TIME TAKES US EVER AWAY…
GREAT LIBERATOR IS. WITH JOLLITY
I CONTEMPLATE ITS VAST SWAY.
AUGURS BEAUTIFULLY TO THE "ON HIGH"
WHEN MEDITATED UPON WITHOUT BIAS,
GIVES HOPE AND INSPIRATION IN A SIGH,
DOES ALL PARTIALITY, INCOMPLETENESS SURPASS.
WELL, THOUGH TIME SEEMS EVER FLEETING,
EVERY INTERCONNECTING MOMENT'S WORK REMAINS.
—YOU SEE? WE'RE NOT JUST HERE FOR THE FLEECING,
BUT FROM EACH UNIQUE MOMENT EACH ONE OF US GAINS…
TIME PASSES, AUGURS WELL!

TIME—A PROFOUND REFLECTION

Composed 2/19/2023. For March 18 Challenge for Nevada Poetry Society, posed by Craig himself. This challenge is to write about Life's Meaning, Purpose, Unity and the Nature of All Reality. The idea is to ponder the greater Nature of Existence and at as Comprehensive a level as one can.

Time
Is a benign and magical Wand
That masterfully
Unites All Conscious Beings,
That includes and subsumes all Places,
All confines and even all Vastnesses of Space…
All diverse yet interrelated phenomena
That exist therein—
Furthermore:
All Beings who are,
Who dwell fixedly attached
To all the diverse Facets
Of this Universal Progression.
Our lives—
That are Many!—
Move through
All well-ordered Stages of Time
As we unfold,
Both Individually and Collectively,
Like a Most Amazing Butterfly
Undergoing its Metamorphosis,
Perfecting its Self-Realization,
Yet with guidance from fellow strivers,
And ever by Grace and Inspiration
From the All-Caring
Supreme Being!
And, thus, we who go forth
are in fact Returning
Back to our all-unifying
Origin Wherein
There Is No End!
Praise God! Amen.

TODAY'S CRUCIAL CHALLENGE—A *RUBAI*

Conceived and revised on 12/30/2021 at home in snow-covered Carson Valley, Nevada – the "Garden Spot of Nevada" that looks up to the Sierras on the West and Pine Nuts on the East.

About what's happening today concerned
Am I! Humanity's gone wild, not learned
Respect or Reverence for All of Life!
—Too much Hubris and Scorn—we need **UPTURN!**

We need to take a serious upswing
Away from ignobility—take wing,
Rise high, attain Life's Grander View,
Perspective that will cause our hearts to Sing!

Because we owe not just ourselves but all
Living creatures and kinds where'er they sprawl
Out o'er all this diverse Amazing Earth
We share as home, wherein relate o'erall!

Today the prideful bubble mankind's made
About's to **BURST**—already is!—as fade
Away, recede we from indulgences
So gross, they're killing Life on Earth—**CHARADE!**

Where is our Savior from our worldly selves?
—I say: it is *within the Self* one delves,
To find this question's burning answer 'pon
Which do depend so many crucial **ELVES!**

Their Realms interrelate in our and all
The Worlds that spin, rotate, *process* and fall
Within patterns that balance, check each one.
—Have Faith! Be of Good Cheer! YOU ARE SAVE-ALL!

Travel Back in Time?

Composed 8/8/2023.

Concerning the reversing—
The journeying backwards in time—
Well, not really—
Yet in memory we can
Revisit past moments,
States and conditions
So as from these to learn…
As recently to me has dawned.

In Time's vast sway,
Its whole and perfect record,
There is a sort of
Repetition of similar situations,
Relations, patterns—common
Threads within Life's Great Tapestry.
Now these are all ones,
About which we must not forget,
But rather return to and face
Again and again,
According to universally
Governing laws and principles
Until we solve all our so-called problems,
Face our ineluctable challenges,
In order to overcome the barriers—
So that our so-called
"Journey back in time"
Can be finally rectified…
All the imperfections…
All the wrongs…
So that we, by grace of God,
Can be again allowed
That noble freedom to most truly advance
And be restored—
Reach all Time's true Goal—
Praise God!

AWESOME, LIFE-CHANGING ENCOUNTER OF MY YOUTH
—Poem to the UFO Entities—for Real!

Composed sometime in mid-2023, this based on the author's true-life experience in the summer of his 13th year. This took place on a hot August day shortly after noon in Minden, Nevada, in 1962.

Meditating upon my experiences and relationships
To those presences operating through so-called UFOs,
I assert that these amazing displays
Truly prove there is a Higher Power…
An overseeing presence
Over all this life and world—
Our present sphere of conscious dwelling.
They are a "tap on the shoulder"
From the Almighty…
A wonderful proof
That someone cares…
Who holds some capacities
Greater than we do ourselves…

Now, a most remarkable experience
Happened one intensely hot August afternoon.
'T was during the summer of my 13th year
In the quaint town of Minden, Nevada.
The heat combined with morning chores
Contributed to my falling into a deep slumber
Upon my comfortable long bed…
After an hour or so amid profound dreams
There arose within my consciousness
A deep and God-like voice
Telling me to "Rise Up!"
"Come Out and Look Up!"
Into the fathomless, cloudless, blue desert sky
Out over the towering cottonwood trees
Toward Minden Park just to the north.
This inwardly sounding voice
Was so replete with beneficence and wisdom
That I trusted it implicitly—without hesitation!

*Photo of UFO's landed in the Southern Nevada Desert (*photo taken and copyright by Craig C Downer, April 29, 2023*)*

Then peering trustingly up to the heavens,
Two resplendently shining silver disks
I beheld there hovering.
And I knew instinctively
That there was a connection
Between them and me.
Remarkably I was transported into
A kind of beautiful, other-worldly spell
Through which came a wonderful message
That had to do with the urgent need
To recognize All Life's True Purpose
Wherefrom True Reverence for Life would spring
From each and every human being.
I experienced an opening up to
A more all-comprehensive view.
This concerned—and still concerns
All life's true, essential nature and
The sheer sentient *beingness*
That we all share!
Praise God! Forever and ever.

Ripples—a *Zen* poem

For challenge by Ann Conibear for February 18, 2023 Nevada Poetry Society meeting.

We are—each individual is!—
Universal in his effects,
Like a stone that's thrown
Into the universal pond of Life
And whose ripples
Reverberate throughout
And in a special way
Touch All!

Craig Carpenter Downer

Meditation Upon Money—a *Zen* poem

Composed January 22, 2023.

In Today's Society
Money as a Medium of Exchange
Has overtaken Common Sense!
Its Association with Obtaining
So many possible Goods and Services—
Whatever one's Fancy or Whim
For getting full "Bang for one's Buck!"—
Has led to a form of Collective Madness
And a Destructiveness that is
Killing Planet Earth!
And so I pray:
Please, dear God,
Deliver us from our fallen state!

POEM TO DEAR BROTHER "BOBBY"
(Robert Gottschalk Downer, né July 6, 1937, Reno, NV, passed on August 31, 2009, Boise, ID.
With his photo as a teenage skier on Mount Rose, just west of Reno, Nevada. Composed on Bobby's
birthday, July 6, 2023.)

Affectionately called Bobby,
My brother meant so many things to me!
A great skier – even champion, far-distance ski jumper –
He set a record that stood for many years.
So patiently he taught me
The art of how to ski.

As civil engineer and land surveyor,
He taught me precise ways to measure,
As did also our dear father – Bob!

So impressive about Bobby
Was his spontaneous,
Original, free and daring spirit!
How often he surprised us
With his unusual wit.
His sense of humor made us laugh,

*"Robert Gottschalk Downer early
1950s by Robert Carpenter Downer,
Bobby's and Craig's father."*

Often noting what seemed
Life's quirkier aspects.

His gift for playing tenor sax
For family or social events was the max.

When out in Nevada desert or California Sierras,
In world of Nature Bobby shone –
Seemed most at home.
Fond of smelling bushes, trees, and flowers,
He also enjoyed discovering native artifacts.

Once he composed a splendid poem
About an ancient desert chief
Whose strong spirit
Spontaneously upon him came.

Now, Bobby was a powerful man,
Nearly six-and-a-half feet tall,
And usually he was all muscle!

Outgoing by nature, he was socially inclined.
He loved church going and
His faith in God was strong!

He didn't give up when times got rough,
but followed through to raise
A fine daughter Julie and son Robert Steve,
Being steadfast in his marriage
Through thick and through thin.

Bobby stood up for the wild horses,
Whose great beauty and spirit of freedom
He greatly admired – and these inspired him!
He confronted those who unjustly made them targets –
Standing up and showing true moral courage!

As a champion college boxer,
He knew how to fight well!
But his final fight in life
Physically laid him low.
I held his left hand,
While his dear wife Marilee held his right,
And dear sister Kay and husband Neil
Were right there at his feet,

When he passed on at Seventy-Two.

It was Leukemia
That he so bravely fought
Until his time for release
From pain and worldly cares had come.
And when this great giant transcended,
An amazing greenish-golden
Light lit up his cozy Boise home –
And far beyond …
The feeling was that of an immense
Relief, release – Return to Heavenly Home!
– Both subtly and tangibly was this conveyed!

And, so, I say: Dear Brother Bobby,
God bless you upon your way …
Your unending journey forth!
And may all your high dreams
For Life come true!
May you realize
All that Life most truly is!
And may God grant you blessed Freedom …
Heavenly scents and your
True Flowering …
Forevermore!
Hallelujah!
　　　*******

END

www.ingramcontent.com/pod-product-compliance
Lightning Source LLC
Chambersburg PA
CBHW042047140726
48006CB00020BA/2571